Top Careers in Two Years

Computers and Information Technology

Titles in the *Top Careers in Two Years* Series

Top Careers in Two Years

Computers and Information Technology

By Claire Wyckoff

Ferguson Publishing
An imprint of Infobase Publishing

Top Careers in Two Years
Computers and Information Technology

Ferguson
An imprint of Infobase Publishing
132 West 31st Street
New York, NY 10001

ISBN-13: 978-0-8160-6903-3
ISBN-10: 0-8160-6903-4

Library of Congress Cataloging-in-Publication Data

Top careers in two years.
    v. cm.
  Includes index.
  Contents: v. 1. Food, agriculture, and natural resources / by Scott Gillam — v. 2. Construction and trades / Deborah Porterfield — v. 3. Communications and the arts / Claire Wyckoff — v. 4. Business, finance, and government administration / Celia W. Seupal — v. 5. Education and social services / Jessica Cohn — v. 6. Health care, medicine, and science / Deborah Porterfield — v. 7. Hospitality, human services, and tourism / Rowan Riley — v. 8. Computers and information technology / Claire Wyckoff — v. 9. Public safety, law, and security / Lisa Cornelio, Gail Eisenberg — v. 10. Manufacturing and transportation — v. 11. Retail, marketing, and sales / Paul Stinson.
    ISBN-13: 978-0-8160-6896-8 (v. 1 : hc : alk. paper)
    ISBN-10: 0-8160-6896-8 (v. 1 : hc : alk. paper)
    ISBN-13: 978-0-8160-6897-5 (v. 2 : hc. : alk. paper)
    ISBN-10: 0-8160-6897-6 (v. 2 : hc. : alk. paper)
    ISBN-13: 978-0-8160-6898-2 (v. 3 : hc : alk. paper)
    ISBN-10: 0-8160-6898-4 (v. 3 : hc : alk. paper)
    ISBN-13: 978-0-8160-6899-9 (v. 4 : hc : alk. paper)
    ISBN-10: 0-8160-6899-2 (v. 4 : hc : alk. paper)
    ISBN-13: 978-0-8160-6900-2 (v. 5 : hc : alk. paper)
    ISBN-10: 0-8160-6900-X (v. 5 : hc : alk. paper)
    ISBN-13: 978-0-8160-6901-9 (v. 6 : hc : alk. paper)
    ISBN-10: 0-8160-6901-8 (v. 6 : hc : alk. paper)
    ISBN-13: 978-0-8160-6902-6 (v. 7 : hc : alk. paper)
    ISBN-10: 0-8160-6902-6 (v. 7 : hc : alk. paper)
    ISBN-13: 978-0-8160-6903-3 (v. 8 : hc : alk. paper)
    ISBN-10: 0-8160-6903-4 (v. 8 : hc : alk. paper)
    ISBN-13: 978-0-8160-6904-0 (v. 9 : hc : alk. paper)
    ISBN-10: 0-8160-6904-2 (v. 9 : hc : alk. paper)
    ISBN-13: 978-0-8160-6905-7 (v. 10 : hc : alk. paper)
    ISBN-10: 0-8160-6905-0 (v. 10 : hc : alk. paper)
    ISBN-13: 978-0-8160-6906-4 (v. 11 : hc : alk. paper)
    ISBN-10: 0-8160-6906-9 (v. 11 : hc : alk. paper)
  1. Vocational guidance—United States. 2. Occupations—United States. 3. Professions—United States.
  HF5382.5.U5T677 2007
  331.7020973—dc22

                                                                                    2006028638

Ferguson books are available at special discounts when purchased in bulk quantities for businesses, associations, institutions, or sales promotions. Please call our Special Sales Department in New York at (212) 967-8800 or (800) 322-8755.

You can find Ferguson on the World Wide Web at http://www.fergpubco.com

Produced by Print Matters, Inc.
Text design by A Good Thing, Inc.
Cover design by Salvatore Luongo

Printed in the United States of America

Sheridan PMI 10 9 8 7 6 5 4 3 2 1

This book is printed on acid-free paper.

Contents

How to Use This Book

This book, part of the *Top Careers in Two Years* series, highlights in-demand careers for readers considering a two-year degree program—either straight out of high school or after working a job that does not require advanced education. The focus throughout is on the fastest-growing jobs with the best potential for advancement in the field. Readers learn about future prospects while discovering jobs they may never have heard of.

An associate's degree can be a powerful tool in launching a career. This book tells you how to use it to your advantage, explore job opportunities, and find local degree programs that meet your needs.

Each chapter provides the essential information needed to find not just a job but a career that fits your particular skills and interests. All chapters include the following features:

- "Vital Statistics" provides crucial information at a glance, such as salary range, employment prospects, education or training needed, and work environment.

- Discussion of salary and wages notes hourly versus salaried situations as well as potential benefits. Salary ranges take into account regional differences across the United States.

- "Keys to Success" is a checklist of personal skills and interests needed to thrive in the career.

- "A Typical Day at Work" describes what to expect at a typical day on the job.

- "Two-Year Training" lays out the value of an associate's degree for that career and what you can expect to learn.

- "What to Look For in a School" provides questions to ask and factors to keep in mind when selecting a two-year program.

- "The Future" discusses prospects for the career going forward.

- "Interview with a Professional" presents firsthand information from someone working in the field.

❧ "Job Seeking Tips" offers suggestions on how to meet and work with people in the field, including how to get an internship or apprenticeship.

❧ "Career Connections" lists Web addresses of trade organizations providing more information about the career.

❧ "Associate's Degree Programs" provides a sampling of some of the better-known two-year schools.

❧ "Financial Aid" provides career-specific resources for financial aid.

❧ "Related Careers" lists similar related careers to consider.

In addition to a handy comprehensive index, the back of the book features two appendices providing invaluable information on job hunting and financial aid. Appendix A, Tools for Career Success, provides general tips on interviewing either for a job or two-year program, constructing a strong résumé, and gathering professional references. Appendix B, Financial Aid, introduces the process of applying for aid and includes information about potential sources of aid, who qualifies, how to prepare an application, and much more.

Introduction

It would be hard to name a phenomenon that has had more impact on the 20th and 21st centuries than digital technology. During the past 50 years, the computer has dramatically changed the way we work, the way we learn, and even the way we socialize. The World Wide Web especially has shaken up our world. The Internet has given us telecommuting, YouTube, MySpace, Amazon, and many other forms of entertainment, communication, and business. What's more, the impact of computer technology has not been limited to a few countries; it has affected every nation in the world. Indeed it has shifted our focus from one that was national to a global perspective.

Nor has the importance of computers diminished in the new millennium. During the past five years, personal computer (PC) sales alone generated $424 billion in revenues in the United States. Month after month new applications and enhancements are developed. Every day, new content is added to the Web, and the amount of online pages grows exponentially.

Although the number of users connecting to the Web probably won't continue increasing as fast in the 21st century as in the 1990s, usage will continue to rise. With a growing population will come more demand for support from Internet service providers (ISPs). There will also be changes in the way we access the Internet, which should produce more demand for wireless connectivity and broadband services. Urban and rural areas will benefit equally from these changes; cities will expand their use of wireless networks, and rural communities will expand their broadband connectivity. As new technological advances are discovered, these also will generate growth since networks will need to upgrade to accommodate them. In addition, so many Web pages are being created that they are not accurately cataloged. A growth of Web search portals in the next decade will be fired by the demand to access this content.

The implications for the job market are obvious. According to the Bureau of Labor Statistics, wages and salaries from employment by Internet service providers, Web search portals, and data processing services are expected to grow 28 percent between 2004 and 2014, twice as fast as the 14 percent projected for the economy as a whole. This growth will differ among industry sectors; the estimated growth from data processing, hosting, and related services is projected at 33 percent with Internet service providers, while Web search portals will grow by 16 percent.

What kinds of professionals will the next decade need? In ISPs and Web search services, computer software engineers, along with network systems and data communications analysts, will probably have the best job opportunities. As companies in the information technology (IT) industry continue to add services and content, they will need these workers to implement the changes.

Among the job titles whose importance will be on the rise in the "networked economy" are the following:

Network Expert: In a recent study by placement agency Robert Half International Consulting, networking was named the most in-demand IT specialty. Of the 1,400 chief information officers surveyed, 32 percent cited networking as the highest-growth area within their IT departments. Because telecommuting and the demand for sharing and accessibility to data are on the rise, the people who understand communications and information at a high and complex level are in more demand than ever before.

Web Programmer/Developer: The demand for these professionals will grow proportionately with the Internet's continued growth. Landing these jobs, however, will require you to be well versed in a variety of programming languages, Java, Cold Fusion, C++, and PERL among them.

Web Site/Database Integrator: According to the Bureau of Labor Statistics, there will be nearly a quarter million job openings in this area within the next 10 years. In addition to standard Web site languages such as HTML, PERL, C++, Java, etc., Web site/database integrators will need to know database languages (like DB2, Oracle, SQL, etc.), and, depending on the systems they inherit, they will need some knowledge of accounting packages and financial and inventory systems. This job also requires an understanding of how to connect databases to an Internet site or an intranet.

Information Architect: Information architects are responsible for learning how users find information on a Web site and for defining the site's organization, navigation, and labeling systems. Courses in Web design may be combined with studies in specific industry environments—health care, financial services, and the like.

The demand for these and other computer specialists to maintain and upgrade the systems that keep users connected and the search engines that make the Web navigable will come from many different sources. Businesses, organizations, and individuals will all increase their use of the Internet to provide information and services. These offerings will range from simple text to retail or subscription video services. Increasing concerns over security also will require more advanced technical solutions, resulting in further job growth within the industry. Both data-hosting services and data-processing centers also should experience a rise in employment as they continue to seek professionals to input paper records into computer files and to convert older, archived data to newer formats.

Ironically, as demand is increasing, the availability of trained IT professionals seems to be on the decline in this country. Recently the Computer Research Association reported on survey results from the Higher Education Research Institute at the University of California at Los Angeles (HERI/UCLA). It indicated that the popularity of computer science (CS) as a major among incoming college freshmen at all undergraduate institutions has dropped significantly in the past four years. Alarmingly, the proportion of women who thought that they might major in CS has fallen to levels unseen since the early 1970s. Indeed, some experts argue that if it were not for outsourcing overseas, the United States would not have enough trained manpower to service its IT industry.

When the U.S. computer industry was young, homeschooled professionals were common. It was possible and not infrequent for would-be jobseekers to get hired on the basis of what they had taught themselves. However, if you think you can get enough experience and get hired today as a result of designing your own Web site or network and reading a lot of manuals, think again. Not only are the systems and applications you'll be required to support much more complex than they were 20 years ago, but the competition for jobs is more intense. So, although an IT job is still very much hands-on, the IT careers of tomorrow are built today by taking courses that lead to degrees and certifications.

A Two-Year Jump Start

For many, a two-year institution is the ideal place to start getting that formal training. Community colleges in particular provide a wide array of technical curricula—offering degrees in computer science, programming, networking, and computer-aided design, among others. Many include courses that prepare students to get certified in particular systems or applications, such as Cisco or Linux.

One of the reasons technical programs at community colleges are so strong is that their faculty tend to be practicing professionals. That means that they usually are aware of the latest industry trends and practices. And they have access to companies that offer internships and other real-world training. One other plus: community college classes are often smaller than those at larger four-year schools, so students receive more personalized instruction.

Also, admission to two-year institutions is not overly competitive. Students are admitted from a wide range of academic backgrounds. So someone who performed below average in high school can excel at a two-year school if they put in the time and energy to their studies.

Another attraction of two-year degrees is that they are more flexible and affordable than traditional four-year programs. Classes are often offered at night, and many programs are now taught via the Internet. The schools are located in geographically convenient areas, so that students can easily live off campus, work full or part time, and commute.

As far as affordability is concerned, the average annual tuition and fees for attending a four-year public school in a student's home state was about $5,130 during the 2004–05 school year, while the tuition to attend a community college was about $2,080, according to a survey by the College Board. Students who attend schools away from home must also pay room and board fees, which at state schools ups the average tally to about $11,350 a year. Still, is the cost of a two-year higher education worth it? Yes, definitely. Students who earn an associate's degree tend to make $2,000 to $6,000 a year more than those who try to get by with just a high school diploma.

Some think that two-year schools lack the traditional college social scene and supportive academic environment. But that is gradually changing—at least 20 percent of two-year colleges provide housing, cafeterias, sports, clubs, and dynamic social activities comparable to what you will find at many four-year schools.

There is plenty of financial aid available at these institutions as well. However, just as with four-year students, two-year students who want a piece of the federal pie usually must complete the Free Application for Federal Student Aid (FAFSA). Private lenders are helping the two-year student, too. For example, SallieMae (http://www.salliemae.com) offers very specific private loans for career training, and U.S. Bank introduced the CampUS Education Loan specifically for those attending two-year schools. (Turn to Appendix B to find out more about financial aid opportunities.)

Is a Computer Technology Career Right for You?

Ask yourself the following questions to see if the careers in this book might be right for you.

- Do you enjoy solving problems?
- Do you have solid math skills, and can you handle advanced mathematical concepts?
- Are you a team player who can take direction from others?
- Do you enjoy working with electronic devices?
- Are you a conscientious worker?
- Are you good with details?
- Do you consider yourself an innovative thinker?
- Can you work long hours on your own?

- Do you have patience and determination?
- Are you dependable (you've missed very few days of school or another job)?
- Can you get along with different personalities?
- Are you a quick thinker?
- Are you flexible about your work schedules? (Would you be willing to work weekends or nights?)

If you answered yes to most of these, then a computer technology career might be for you.

Finding the Right School

A good place to start your search for a two-year college that fits your needs is online at http://www.collegeboard.com. You can key in specific criteria, such as the program you want to study or the area where you want to live, and it'll display options that meet your needs. You also can find information about colleges at libraries, which usually have college directories and individual catalogs. When you find a college that piques your interest, check out its Web site, look over its catalog, and talk to someone at the school. If the school is nearby, you may even want to visit its campus to get a feel for the place.

When choosing a school, look for one that's accredited by professional associations in your field. Unfortunately, some so-called diploma mills run fraudulent programs: They hand out worthless diplomas and certificates without teaching students the skills they need to work in their chosen professions. To learn more about such fraudulent schools, check "Diploma Mills and Accreditation" at the U.S. Department of Education's Web site: http://www.ed.gov/students/prep/college/diplomamills/index.html. The Council for Higher Education Accreditation also offers helpful information at http://www.chea.org.

The best way to avoid such pitfalls is to enroll in accredited schools and programs. The following are top accrediting agencies for schools:

- Accrediting Council for Independent Colleges and Schools (http://www.acics.org)
- Distance Education and Training Council   (http://www.detc.org)
- Middle States Association of Colleges and Schools (http://www.msacs.org)
- New England Association of Schools and Colleges (http://www.neasc.org/)
- North Central Association of Colleges and Schools (http://www.ncahigherlearningcommission.org/)

☞ Northwest Association of Schools and Colleges
(http://www.opi.state.mt.us/nascu/text.htm)

☞ Southern Association of Colleges and Schools   (http://www.sacs.org)

☞ Western Association of Schools and Colleges   (http://
www.wascweb.org)

If you think there's a chance you might want to continue your school-ing, make sure that most of the credits you earn in a two-year program can be transferred to a four-year school. Someone learning to be a computer programmer, for example, can continue training to become a computer software designer with more responsibility and a higher paycheck.

IT Contacts

For general information on IT and computer-related careers, contact the following:

Association for Computing Machinery, 2 Penn Plaza, Suite 701, New York, New York 10121-0701   (http://www.acm.org)

IEEE (Institute of Electrical and Electronics Engineers) Computer Society, 1730 Massachusetts Avenue N.W., Washington, D.C. 20036-1992   (http://www.computer.org/portal/site/ieeecs/index.jsp)

Network Professional Association, 1401 Hermes Lane, San Diego, California 92154   (http://www.npanet.org)

Association of Information Technology Professionals, 401 North Michigan Avenue, Suite 2400, Chicago, Illinois 60611-4267 (http://www.aitp.org)

The Computing Technology Industry Association, 1815 S. Meyers Road, Suite 300, Oakbrook Terrace, Illinois 60181-5228 (http://www.comptia.org)

Computer Programmer

Vital Statistics

Salary: Computer programmers earn a median annual income of almost $63,000, although the lowest earners made just $35,000, according to 2006 figures from the U.S. Bureau of Labor Statistics.

Employment: Competition is intense for jobs in this field, and growth is projected to fall below the average for other occupations through 2014 due to outsourcing.

Education: The associate's degree is a widely used entry-level credential for prospective computer programmers. In 2004, two thirds of all programmers had college degrees.

Work Environment: Programmers generally work in offices in comfortable surroundings.

If you're into interactive media—games, video, etc.—you have computer programmers to thank. Programmers are the people who convert the specifications and designs of software engineers and systems analysts into the logical instructions that computers follow. Many programmers also update, repair, modify, and expand existing programs; prepare reports on the status of software; or assist with the collection of documentation and the development of software specifications.

Although the programs these workers create may be so simple they can be written in a few hours, programs that use complex mathematical formulas, such as Bombelli (a powerful viewer for complex functions, written in Java), may require over a year of work. Depending on the position, the responsibilities and educational backgrounds of programmers vary widely.

Programmers fall into two main categories: applications programmers and systems programmers. Applications programmers write programs to handle specific jobs, such as a program to track inventory at a CD store. Applications programmers also revise packaged software or customize generic applications to meet the specific needs of their companies. Systems programmers, in contrast, write programs to maintain and control computer systems software, such as operating systems, like Linux, networked systems (LANs and WANs), database systems, and customer support systems. These programmers make changes in the instructions that tell the network, workstations, and central processing units of the computer system how to handle the various jobs. Their programs tell computers how to communicate with terminals, printers, and disk drives. Because they must understand an entire computer system, these programmers often assist applications programmers when they search for the source of a problem.

The interactive media developer is a very specific type of programmer. These experts perform some or all of the following:

- program animation software for interactive CDs, DVDs, video game cartridges and Internet-based applications
- program special effects software for film and video applications
- write, modify, integrate and test software code for e-commerce and other Internet applications
- perform other support functions related to interactive media or e-commerce

Programmers are multilinguists. To code the instructions, they must be fluent in programming languages, artificial intelligence languages, or advanced "object-oriented" languages. Programmers are often referred to by the languages they know (e.g., Java programmers). The more languages programmers know, the more likely they are to find work and get ahead in their careers. Besides Java, examples of some currently popular languages are C++ and Perl.

Programmers are used in nearly every industry, but the majority work for companies that provide computer systems design and related services. Other industries that depend on programmers are telecommunications, software publishing, finance, insurance, education, and government.

Since learning new languages is important to career success, most programmers continue their education after they earn their degrees. Although the demand for programmers is expected to be on the rise through at least 2014, programming will become so specialized that anyone with less than a two-year degree will face strong competition for jobs. Learning a variety of programming languages and tools for networking, database management, and Internet applications will increase your chances of landing one.

On the Job

As a programmer you'll usually work in an office, although you may work occasionally from home. Almost every industry employs programmers, but the largest concentration is in computer systems design and related services. Large numbers of programmers also work for telecommunications companies, software publishers, financial firms, insurance carriers, educational institutions, and government agencies.

A lot of the time, programmers work together in teams that are supervised by a senior programmer or project manager. They may be required to work long hours to meet deadlines and resolve unexpected problems. And spending long hours working at the computer can lead to health problems such as eyestrain, backaches, and wrist problems.

Nowadays, businesses often outsource computer programming, and even locally programmers may work as contracted employees or independent consultants. These freelancers provide expertise on new programming languages or specialized applications. But once their job is completed, they move onto or search for the next assignment. Typically, employers do not take on freelancers as permanent employees.

> ## "Be nice to nerds. Chances are you'll end up working for one."
> —Bill Gates, founder and chairman, Microsoft Corporation

Keys to Success

To be a successful computer programmer, you need
- good math skills
- analytical and logical thinking
- patience
- creativity
- problem-solving ability
- attention to detail
- communication skills

Do You Have What It Takes?

When hiring programmers, employers look first to be sure candidates have the latest programming skills. The number and type of languages you know will usually determine where you work and at what level. Your ultimate success, however, will also require you to be able to think logically and pay close attention to detail. Programming calls for patience, persistence, and the ability to analyze data under pressure. Ingenuity and creativity are important when you are expected to design solutions and test work for potential failures. For systems programmers, the ability to both work with abstract concepts and do technical analysis is vital because they work with essential software that controls a computer's operation. Because programmers are expected to work in teams and at times interact directly with users, employers prefer programmers who are able to communicate well with other programmers as well as with nontechnical personnel.

A Typical Day at Work

When you first start as a programmer, all your day-to-day tasks are planned out for you. Entry-level or junior programmers may work alone on simple assignments after some initial instruction, or they may be assigned to work on a team with more experienced programmers. Either way, they usually work under close supervision. Once past that point, programming is actually only half the story. On a typical day, these professionals may slog though a mountain of administrative, procedural, and even political tasks before digging into the actual code writing.

For a regular programmer, the day generally starts with group planning. This means attending meetings or teleconferencing. Communications skills become critical since you have to listen closely and pitch in when coworkers ask for your technical advice. Many programmers find this an especially interesting part of the job because they get to interface with other departments and help shape the end product.

With planning come the limitations of budget, manpower, and a constant dose of reality. Programmers constantly rely on their creativity and problem-solving skills to make a project work under budget limitations. Decisions depend a lot on the environment. When creating a high-traffic Web site, you need to favor performance. When creating a banking application, you need to emphasize stability and security.

After meetings and planning, programmers may turn to the nitty-gritty of hardware and software work. As budgets shrink, tech-job responsibilities have been merged. Since larger companies often require their applications to be built to fit specific systems, programmers must know the server and hardware needs of their systems. When these professionals sit down to do the actual programming, all the data structures, control loops, and system protocols they learned in Computer Science 101 come into practical use. However, each new task can bring new problems that college has not prepared you for. This is another time when good communications skills come in handy. If you can work well with a team, brainstorming can lead you to a perfect solution.

How to Break In

One of the best things you can do while you're in school is fool around with computers. There's no substitute for experience. The more comfortable you are with programming, the better you'll get. Try to learn as much as you can about many programming languages and be *very* proficient at one or two. If you can't get paid for it, do it yourself at home.

Certification is a way to demonstrate a level of competence and may provide you with a competitive advantage. Voluntary certification is available through various professional organizations. In addition to earning a language-specific certificate, you may have to pass a vendor's and software firm's certification process, demonstrating your mastery of a specific product.

Two-Year Training

If you want to concentrate mostly on the theory and design of computer systems, consider a major in computer science. But if you want to dive right into learning the computer languages, like C++ and Java, that run operating systems, networks, and software, computer programming could be the major for you. Computer programming majors learn how to write in various programming languages used for software development and operating systems. Topics covered include program testing, debugging, and customization.

Typically a programming major will study business communications, C++ programming, database design, database essentials, Java programming, networking essentials, programming fundamentals, Visual Basic programming, and Web programming. Many schools require a *capstone*, or final project. This is a great chance to show your stuff when faced with a realistic business situation. Working with a team of other students, you'll design, program, test, and put into practice a complete software solution. You'll get little support from instructors, and the experience is great preparation for the working world.

What to Look For in a School

When considering a two-year school, be sure to ask these questions:

☞ Does the program teach the most up-to-date applications?

☞ Are professors currently working in the profession and well versed in the latest technology?

☞ Will you be able to take online classes in addition to classroom lectures?

☞ Will the program help you find work after graduation?

☞ Does the program offer certificates or diplomas in specialized areas of programming?

Did You Know?

In 1949, the language Short Code appeared, according to Byte.com. It was the first computer language for electronic devices, and it required the programmer to change its statements into 0s and 1s by hand.

Interview with a Professional: Q&A

Laurie Quinn

Senior information systems consultant, Boston, Massachusetts

Q: *How did you get started?*

A: I started programming right after graduation. I interviewed with a local manufacturer who was impressed by the effort I put in working my way through school. I had a paper route at 13 that I kept through college, and I also worked at a local country store. I struggled for three years working two jobs, doing various things like retail clerk, manager, landscaper, and worked in a garden shop. With some networking, a bit of confidence, and good timing, I was offered a job at a computer consulting company. I now work for a large health care company that has given me some great opportunities to grow my career.

Q: *What's a typical day like?*

A: Currently very hectic with juggling a few assignments. I am involved with a team that is currently converting our U.S. HR [human resources] system on to a global platform, which means many meetings and putting many plans into action. I take care of daily conference calls and e-mails with our global counterparts, and I travel for meetings when needed. I work with a great bunch of people who will help each other whenever needed.

Q: *What's your advice for those starting a career?*

A: You have to work hard to prove yourself, and it doesn't matter where you are in your career, you always need to work at it. Take pride in what you do, and you will find you will do it better. There will be times you need to speak up for yourself, so pick your battles—be firm but polite. Respect yourself and others—you never know who may be your manager one day. Challenge yourself to take a risk and don't be afraid to make mistakes. Just learn from them and move on. Always be willing to learn something new; be flexible and be open-minded. Don't wait for your manager to approach you; approach them and ask for more opportunities. Managers appreciate someone stepping up, and it will show your superiors you are a go-getter. This will give you the visibility you need to get the sought-after projects and also to get that promotion. Above all, *believe in yourself.*

(continued on next page)

(continued from previous page)

Q: *What's the best part of being a programmer?*

A: The gratification of knowing I created something that will be used by someone somewhere in the world that makes their daily life a little easier. Programmers need to think logically with algorithms and math, but we are also very creative. We take a blank paper or screen and we create an amazing combination of letters, numbers, and graphics that are used by people who make this world run. I've done well with my two-year associate's degree and appreciate the paycheck, but I never take it for granted. I've learned that companies can morph into three different names at different times with completely different foc[i] and priorities. The job you had yesterday may not be the same job you are doing today, and you never even left your cubicle. You have to roll with it and embrace the ever-changing world to succeed in this field.

The Future

Computer sectors requiring design and software services will be among the most rapidly growing sectors of the U.S. economy over the next decade. In addition, there will be new demand for programmers to the extent evolving technologies require companies to adapt to new language and computer systems. Video games and competitive Web sites like Google will all eagerly snatch up versatile programmers, although downside pressures on domestic employment in this area are felt due to outsourcing.

The growth rate of programming jobs, therefore, is not expected to exceed that for specialists in other computer-related fields. Changing technology is affecting the scope of programmers' responsibilities, reducing the need for manual work. An increase in the use of software packages and the ability of users to write their own programs will also reduce the need for programmers.

Job Seeking Tips

Follow the suggestions below and turn to Appendix A for tips on résumés and interviewing.

✔ Know which industries are hiring.

✔ Learn new skills to put on your résumé.

✔ Before an interview, research the company.

✔ Expect to be tested.

✔ Be prepared for hands-on exercises.

✔ Follow up after every interview.

Career Connections

For more on careers in computer programming, contact the following organizations.

National Association of Computer Programmers http://www .napusa.org

Association for Computing Machinery http://www.acm.org

Association of Information Technology Professionals http://www.aitp.org

IEEE Computer Society http://www.computer.org/portal/site/ieeecs/index.jsp

Associate's Degree Programs

Here are a few two-year schools offering quality computer programming programs:

Wake Technical Community College, Raleigh, North Carolina

Bristol Community College, Fall River, Massachusetts

Lane Community College, Eugene, Oregon

Seminole Community College, Sanford, Florida

Financial Aid

Here are a few scholarships related to computer programming. For more on financial aid for two-year students, turn to Appendix B.

Microsoft Scholarship Program Microsoft offers about $500,000 a year to help foster future computer scientists.   http://www .microsoft.com/college/ss_overview.mspx

Hispanic College Fund/Google Scholarship Program This is for those who plan on going beyond a two-year degree and want to earn a master's in computer science.   http://scholarships.hispanicfund.org

Institute of Electrical and Electronics Engineers Scholarships http://www.ieee.org/students

Related Careers

Computer software engineer, computer scientist, database administrator, computer systems analysts, statistician, mathematician, engineer, and operations research analyst.

Computer-Aided Drafter and Designer

Vital Statistics

Salary: Computer-aided drafters and designers work full-time, salaried positions that pay on average $40,000 to $43,000 a year, depending on specialty, according to 2006 figures from the U.S. Bureau of Labor Statistics.

Employment: Employment of computer-aided drafters and designers is expected to grow slower than the average for all occupations through 2014 because drafters tend to work in industries—like car making—that are in decline.

Education: Two years of postsecondary training in computer-aided drafting and design (CADD) provides the strong technical skills needed to gain employment in this field.

Work Environment: Common work settings include factories, educational institutions, health care facilities, businesses, government, and consulting firms.

If you've got a passion for computers and an interest in architecture or engineering, computer-aided drafting and design (CADD) is a career area with real growth potential. CADD breaks down into two big categories: architectural and mechanical. Its end results are all around. Virtually every building and man-made environment you see today was first conceived using CADD—from residences and commercial office space to sports stadiums and public parks. CADD is also used to design tools and machinery. Industries as varied as aerospace engineering, landscape architecture, and jewelry depend on CADD to produce their products. From toasters to space shuttles—they all had a start in CADD.

This type of design is not new technology. The aerospace and automotive industries developed their own software packages to assist product design and development more 40 years ago. Commercial CADD systems have been available since 1964. These early systems, however, used expensive mainframe computers that only the largest companies could afford. Advances in computer technology and software have brought CADD to far more users. Now, CADD experts apply their skills in specialized areas, creating furniture, toys, sports equipment, vehicles, medical tools, housewares, and heavy equipment such as tractors and cranes. CADD enables designers to churn out fast and accurate drawings, and it lends flexibility to change drawings with minimal effort. In effect, these designers lay out their products on-screen, viewing them in a three-dimensional (3-D) format. In the computer, they can tinker with their creations and make corrections to the specifications. Once their plans are finalized, designers forward their instructions to production. Designs typically include details on dimensions, materials, and procedures.

With the simpler forms of CADD, a drafter, working from an engineer's or architect's rough sketch, produces drawings on a computer screen. Plans can be sketched out using low-end software like Adobe Illustrator or on high-end software like Alias. Keyboards, graphics tablets, digitizers, and light pens have replaced the pens, inks, compasses, and other tools that drafters relied on for generations. Now instead of drawing a line of ink on paper, the CADD expert makes a glowing line on a video console.

Through a series of programmed commands, the drafter can produce finished drawings in much less time and of a higher quality than those produced by hand. When products are developed in 3-D, detail designers depend on software such as AutoCAD, Solid Works, Alias, Vellum, and Pro E. Using the final CADD files, designers can produce actual models of their 3-D images with rapid prototyping tools such as wax deposition and stereolithography.

On the Job

As an entry-level or junior drafter, you'll probably do routine work under close supervision. At the intermediate level, you'll be expected to exercise more judgment and perform more complex calculations when preparing and modifying drawings. To advance, a strong knowledge of engineering and manufacturing can help. In addition, you'll rely on good interpersonal skills in working directly with engineers, surveyors, architects, other professionals, and, sometimes, customers themselves.

Obviously you'll be working with computers since they play a central role in the job—but the job's not all about sitting behind a screen in an office. If you're working in civil engineering on the construction of a bridge, for example, you may go out in the field to visualize how designs will fit into the landscape and verify measurements.

For the most part, you can expect to work a 40-hour workweek (including some evenings). Common work settings include factories, educational institutions, health care facilities, business and government offices, and consulting firms.

In a smaller design consulting firm, or if you freelance, you'll probably adjust your workdays to suit your clients' schedules and deadlines. In these situations, you may tend to work longer hours and in smaller, more congested environments. You may work in your own firm's office or studio or in clients' offices. Drafters usually work in comfortable offices furnished with new computers that are fast enough to do the required assignments. Because they spend long periods in front of computer terminals doing detailed work, drafters may be subject to eyestrain, back discomfort, and hand and wrist problems.

Keys to Success

To succeed in a career using CADD, you should have

- attention to detail
- the ability to sit and focus for long periods of time
- interest in how things are put together
- team-playing skills
- good vision
- good fine-motor skills
- some aptitude for drawing and design

Do You Have What It Takes?

You will need to have good communication skills, a passion for problem solving, and an interest in art and design—and have a good understanding of construction methods and processes. Mechanical ability and visual aptitude also are important. Prospective drafters should be able to draw well and perform detailed work accurately and neatly. Artistic ability is helpful in some specialized fields, as is knowledge of manufacturing and construction methods.

How to Break In

Employers seek drafters who have taken postsecondary courses and have gotten the training in design or drafting offered by many two-year technical institutes and community colleges. Applicants are especially in demand if they have well-honed drafting and mechanical-drawing skills; knowledge of drafting standards, mathematics, science, and engineering technology; and, of course, a solid background in CADD techniques.

The American Design Drafting Association (ADDA) has established a certification program for drafters. Although employers usually do not require certification, the understanding of nationally recognized practices and standards can boost a job seeker's appeal. Individuals who wish to become certified must pass the Drafter Certification Test, which is administered periodically at ADDA-authorized sites. Applicants are tested on basic drafting concepts, such as geometric construction, working drawings, and architectural terms.

A Typical Day at Work

A CADD professional's day depends on his or her specialty—whether it be electronics and wiring diagrams, civil engineering, architecture, machinery and mechanical devices, or pipelines. The average drafter juggles a number of responsibilities during the course of the day or the duration of a project. These tasks may include generating computerized sketches of a product idea, building rough models of what the product might look like, and presenting ideas to clients or potential customers who might buy the finished product. CADD experts learn about all the technology that goes into the product, and they often conduct research on how a customer may use the product. When mechanical drafters finalize a design and specifications, they send files to the manufacturers, who follow them to produce the product. These professionals pay visits to material suppliers and manufacturers to inspect how the product production and assembly is working. They also conduct follow-up studies to see if a new product is working as expected.

Meetings can eat up a large part of the day. They're held either in-house to review what needs to be done or at client sites to discuss their needs. Sometimes designers assume the role of art director, brainstorming with a copywriter or a team of "creatives." A notebook must always be within reach to sketch and jot down ideas. When meetings wrap up, designers fix themselves in front of their computers (Macs tend to be favored). Here, they get down to the business of real designing. Finished files get backed up to the company's network so they are readily available and identifiable to everyone involved.

Two-Year Training

Community colleges offer curricula similar to those in technical institutes but include more courses on theory and liberal arts. A typical CADD program will include courses on mathematics and the use of CADD software. Students learn to create drawings, plans, and computer models used to construct buildings or manufacture products. Courses include architectural drafting, building codes, business and technical writing, computer-aided drafting, construction materials, engineering-design graphics, machine drafting, product design, communications, and technical drawing.

CADD majors specialize in different areas, so their studies vary accordingly. An electronics drafter, for example, will master electronic components and circuit drawing. The architectural CADD student may design a small home as an assignment and complete a set of working drawings that carpenters and other construction workers would follow to build the house.

What to Look For in a School

When evaluating a two-year program, ask the following:

☞ Which does the program stress more—the theories and fundamentals of drafting or the latest technologies?

☞ What types of computer software and hardware are used in the courses?

☞ Are the software and hardware up-to-date?

☞ Is the software widely used in key industries?

☞ Is the software used in the industry or geographic location in which you'd like to work?

☞ What kinds of jobs are obtained by the school's graduates?

☞ What are the faculty's qualifications?

☞ Is the program certified by the American Design Drafting Association?

The Future

According to the U.S. Department of Labor, employment of computer-aided drafters and designers is expected to grow somewhat slower than the average for all occupations through 2014 because of concentration of CADD work in declining industries. Still, the needs of industry generally and increasingly complex design problems associated with new products and manufacturing processes will increase the demand for computer-aided design services. Further, computer-aided designers are increasingly doing more work traditionally performed by engineers and architects, which increases the demand.

As technology continues to advance, employers will look for drafters with a strong background in fundamental drafting principles, a high level of technical sophistication, and the ability to apply their knowledge to a broader range of responsibilities. Growth is expected to be greatest for mechanical, architectural, and civil engineering drafters. Demand for particular drafting specialties varies throughout the country because employment usually is contingent on the needs of local industry.

> ## "'CADD' may represent the greatest increase in productivity since electricity."
> **—The National Science Foundation**

Interview with a Professional:
Q&A

Jeffrey Briseno

Civil engineering–CADD designer, architectural and
engineering CADD adjunct professor, Austin Community
College, Austin, Texas

Q: *How did you get started?*

A: In 1996, while working on a drawing project at Austin Community College, my instructor Doug Smith, approached me with a job posting from a civil engineering firm that was in need of a CADD technician. He picked me for my attention to detail and the quality of drawings. So, I interviewed for the position and got the job with just the few drawings that I had completed in class. Fortunately, being a quality student opened the door to start my career as a CADD drafter. I got other jobs with a quality drawing portfolio, a vast array of software skill sets [related to the job], and the ability to communicate to the firm why it would benefit if it hired me. I now also work as a part-time college professor teaching CADD drafting at the same college I got my degree from. This proved to be the one of the best career moves I could have made. It allows me to stay up-to-date on the latest software releases and advance my skills.

Q: *What's a typical day like?*

A: In my case, a typical day involves first meeting with the engineer and/or design team to discuss the pressing issues of the day, such as job priority, drawing deadlines, design parameters, and assigning duties to the appropriate personnel. Basically, we figure up our "plan of attack" for that day. This process also allows us to keep everything in front of us and maintain organization. Once I have my assignments, I work on the drawings at my workstation. The hard part is trying to figure out which music CD I want to listen to while I work!

Every now and then I will answer a call to help a client who may be wondering how a project is coming along or someone who is trying to get information on what is involved in getting a project started. Interruptions are very common. Sometimes we will have to switch from one job to another for various emergency reasons. So, that's where 10 deep relaxing breaths really help, to avoid turning into the Incredible Hulk. Once I'm done with a drawing I will present a rough to the engineer for review. If he comes back with a "red-line" markup, I'll make the revisions and print a final set of plans. I turn them over to a supervisor for one final review and then they are submitted to the client. At the end of the day, we account for the time spent on each job and try to get those 10 songs out of our heads that we were listening to all day.

Q: *What's your advice for those starting a career?*

A: My advice for those starting a new CADD career is to always do quality drawings. Make sure your line work is perfect and it is visually pleasing— doing so may get you in the door. But proficiency of skills with the software of choice is mandatory. Your employer doesn't care how pretty the drawings are if it takes too long to produce them. Remember, be an asset, not a liability.

Q: *What's the best part of being a designer?*

A: The best part of being a designer is that each day is a new challenge. You get to work with people who are very creative, and it allows you to continue to grow and evolve your own skills and abilities every day. The pay is pretty good too.

Did You Know?

Mechanical engineering students at the University of California, Berkeley, create "smart" mechanical engineering products using computer-aided drafting and design (CADD) software. Inventions have included a portable vaccine injector, robotic fish for underwater exploration, a golf trolley, and a mapping robot.

Job Seeking Tips

See the suggestions below and turn to Appendix A for advice on résumés and interviewing.

✔ Analyze your skills, interests and motivations.

✔ Explore types of jobs to find out about entry requirements, salaries, and working conditions.

✔ Find out which job sectors have the greatest need for CADD professionals.

✔ Volunteer your services or work as an intern to develop your portfolio and skills.

✔ Network by participating in professional organizations and attending professional seminars and conferences.

Career Connections

For more information on CADD careers, contact the following organizations.

Association for Computer Aided Design in Architecture http://www.acadia.org

Facility Information Council of National Institute of Building Sciences http://www.nibs.org

CAD Society http://www.cadsociety.com

American Design and Drafting Association http://www.adda.org

CAD Digest http://www.caddigest.com

American Society of Mechanical Engineers http://www.asme.org

CADD/GIS Technology Center https://tsc.wes.army.mil/default.asp

The Institute of Electrical and Electronics Engineers http://www.ieee.org

American Institute of Architects http://www.aiaonline.com

Associate's Degree Programs

Here are a few schools with well-regarded CADD training programs:

Austin Community College, Austin, Texas

Arapahoe Community College, Littleton, Colorado

Coffeyville Community College, Coffeyville, Kansas

Spokane Community College, Spokane, Washington

Wytheville Community College, Wytheville, Virginia

Hartford Community College, Bel Air, Maryland

Montgomery County Community College, Pottstown, Pennsylvania

Financial Aid

Here are a couple CADD-related scholarships. Note that two-year colleges such as Joliet Junior College in Illinois, offer their own CADD scholarships. For more on financial aid for two-year students, turn to Appendix B.

American Architectural Foundation Minority/Disadvantaged Scholarship Amounts range from $500 to $2,500 and are determined by financial need.   http://www.archfoundation.org/aaf/aaf/Programs.Fellowships.htm

Flexographic Technical Association Fund Flexography Scholarship This award gives $2,000 to high school seniors who are interested in pursuing a degree in flexography—a kind of industrial design used to print labels and packaging. Applicants must have a minimum 3.0 GPA, and show academic excellence, particularly in the graphic design area. http://www.flexography.org/online/education/scholarship_info.cfm

Related Careers

Architects, engineers, engineering technicians; science technicians, cartographers, photogrammetrists, surveyors, and surveying technicians.

Webmaster

Vital Statistics

Salary: The average starting salary for a Webmaster is $42,000 per year, according to 2006 data from U.S. Bureau of Labor Statistics.

Employment: Very fast job growth (surpassing that of other occupations) is expected through at least 2014, according to the Bureau of Labor Statistics.

Education: A two-year degree in Web management, Web design and administration, computer science, technical communication, graphic design, or even marketing can lead to success in this career.

Work Environment: Webmasters generally work in offices or computer labs or even their homes.

Most people you know probably go online at least once a day. After all, you have to at least check your daily e-mails. And beyond mail, the Web offers at least 76 million Web sites, according to *WebUser* magazine. Increasingly, sites are more entertaining and interactive—from YouTube to Amazon to Google. They want to keep your attention just like a movie or a TV show.

To put it simply, Webmasters build these sites. Creating sites that are both useful and dynamic requires a unique combination of artistic skill and computer savvy. Webmasters bring together these talents in a career that's challenging, creative, and continually changing.

The specific tasks involved in Web building and administration include the following:

- Information architecture—planning how the content will be managed and displayed
- Web design—creating and laying out the visual images and coding the content
- Web development—dealing with the more sophisticated Web sites that handle online inquiries, search engine optimization, and Web hosting
- Account or project management—coordinating all these functions over several sites.

Depending on the scope of the site, each of these jobs may be done by different individuals or teams, or they may be handled by one individual. Masters rely on some basic software and programming to give computers instructions for how words and graphics should look on the screen. They may build different versions of a site to adapt it to the needs of different kinds of computers. They may try to make a site work faster by keeping the size of files as small as possible to minimize download time.

Webmasters place all the content, graphics, and user tools on the pages. If a business Web site allows online purchases, the master installs the tool that lets customers give their credit card numbers. To make sure everything works right, Webmasters test all the pages and functions. They observe people using the sites to see if any parts are hard to use. Links may not work; pictures may not show up. If difficulties arise, Webmasters are ready to fix them. They also spend a lot of time updating established sites. If someone clicks on a site that isn't working or is out-of-date, he or she most likely will click away to another URL (uniform resource locator), which, more simply put, is a Web address. (For example, http://www.allwebjobs.com is a URL—a Web jobs board.)

Currently, the more widely used software applications among Webmasters are Dreamweaver and Web Fusion. However, Webmasters usually know several different programs. They create sites by typing direct instructions in hypertext markup language (HTML) or use Perl, C++, Java, or JavaScript.

In addition to site construction, these professionals figure out where to store Web site information. (Usually, sites reside on a big computer called a server. Companies and individuals may pay another company called a "Web host" to store their sites.)

In today's technologically driven culture, opportunities for Webmasters are virtually infinite. The kinds of business that frequently employ Webmasters include media companies, computer software development firms, and information technology consulting firms. Large corporations often split the workload for their sites into specific tasks, each requiring its own team of specialists, overseen by the Webmaster. Here, the Webmaster also is expected to hire and supervise personnel in such Web-related positions as graphic design, programming, marketing, Internet security, and advertising.

On the Job

Webmasters may work for one employer or for several companies as contracted employees. They usually work in offices or computer labs or from their home computers. Some new media companies place great value on keeping their Web gurus happy on the job so they provide workers with a fridge-full of cold beverages, a pool table, and even a friendly dog to play with when they need a break.

As employees, Internet professionals usually work a 40-hour week, Monday to Friday, but sometimes they log long hours, especially when there's a tight deadline or a sudden problem. Most Webmasters thrive on problem solving and computer puzzles. They also like the creativity involved in launching and maintaining Web sites. It can often be a solitary job, but interaction with clients and coworkers is often needed to hash out new ideas. The job may not appear to be hazardous, but sitting in front of a computer screen for long hours each day can hurt backs, wrists, and eyes.

> **"Give a person a fish and you feed them for a day; teach that person to use the Internet and they won't bother you for weeks."**
> —Author unknown

Keys to Success

To be a successful Webmaster, you need
- creativity and imagination
- good written and verbal skills
- a passion for computers
- good knowledge of how the internet works
- problem-solving skills
- ability to meet deadlines
- solid team-playing ability

Do You Have What It Takes?

If you love surfing the Web and wonder what makes your favorite sites special, this may be the field for you. As this career continues to morph, so does the job description. While skills vary, pros rely on a unique blend of technical and creativity abilities. You definitely should have an interest in computer science and programming. Strong writing skills are valued as companies want their "Web heads" to post information that is concise and captivating. To land a job in this field, an interest in advertising can help, too, since many firms use their sites to sell and advertise. Math and science classes give you the practice needed for solving problems, and English can develop your communication abilities.

How to Break In

Originally, all you needed to become a Webmaster was a computer, access to an Internet service provider (ISP), and some simple programming skills or a "what you see is what you get" (WYSIWYG) Web page program. Today, the World Wide Web is big business, and the job market has grown as dramatically as the Web itself. To break in, you'll need to become proficient with the Web design programs and languages (such as HTML, Flash, Dreamweaver, Shockwave, Javascript, and Perl).

There is no substitute for experience. While official training in a two-year program will give you a foundation of marketable skills, you need to show you can do it yourself. Start by building your own simple Web site, visiting Web sites (with a critical eye), and reading about Web design and usability issues.

By the time you begin interviewing, you should have built at least one site. If you can't get paid for it, volunteer to construct a Web site for an organization. You may want to work toward Webmaster certification—several community colleges offer certification and it can even be earned through online courses.

A Typical Day at Work

Your day begins with an immediate visit to your Web site. You really can't get going unless you're sure your site is up, in action, and looking the way it should. Certain pages will be more important than others, and you may take a few minutes to read through these carefully. If there's any new information that's scheduled for release on a certain day, your next task will be to push it out from the "development server" to the "live Web server." Then, that information is available to the public.

After all that is done, you'll probably check your e-mail. Most Webmasters use at least two monitors: one to look at the site, and the other to handle e-mails. On a typical day a Webmaster can answer as many as 150 e-mails. After e-mail comes voicemail. But once you tend to messages, it's down to business. While you spend some time designing and writing material for your site, you devote even more hours to problems that users have found. You check a log to see what new incidents have been reported.

Meetings can also consume a lot of your day. You may have to meet with departments, such as advertising, that would like to have a greater Web presence. Meetings define what the goals for the site are, and how proposed changes fit in with the established site. You'll need to address expectations about incorporating some of the whiz-bang, nifty stuff that can't happen overnight. Still, you and coworkers all agree that the Web site will be more dynamic with some Flash animation and a banner ad on top of each page.

Another meeting later in the day covers company-wide projects that require Web announcements and possibly a page or two, but no real presence. You find out the scope of the projects and outline how you'll handle these needs.

Two-Year Training

There are several different educational approaches toward becoming a Webmaster, but you will need a well-rounded education for designing, operating, troubleshooting, and maintaining Web sites. A strong associate's degree program in Web design and administration emphasizes computer skills but also cultivates a sense of layout and design, as well as basic business and marketing skills. Most programs teach at least HTML, the basic computer language for the creation of Web pages, but courses may include training in Spy, Java, Visual Basic, and Perl. The Web is a visual medium, so classes in graphics teach the elements of design, color theory, and layout. Photography courses, where you can learn many of the same principles, are also an option. You should also be aware of copyright law, and how it affects what graphics you may use on your site.

Business courses, as well as writing, editing, and proofreading courses, are especially important for anyone who wants to freelance. Not only will you need to speak with clients, but also to keep your own records straight. Both writing and business courses will help you decide what portion of the copy will become body copy and which should be headlines or hyperlinks.

Some schools offer a Web management major. In this program, you'll learn the basics of networking and the best ways to ensure site security. You'll also learn the technical skills needed to maintain sites and servers and practice evaluating and improving Web sites for maximum user-friendliness and marketability. Other degrees that can lead to success as a Webmaster are in computer science, technical communications, graphics, and marketing, to name just a few.

What to Look For in a School

When considering a two-year school, be sure to ask these questions:

☞ Are there any computer programs or skills you should learn before starting the program? It may help to get a handle on basic computer applications or Web design, for example.

☞ Check out the labs. Are they equipped with the latest computer hardware and software?

☞ Does the school maintain partnerships with industry leaders?

☞ Is there an internship program or other opportunities for real-world experience?

☞ Are classes small enough for individualized help?

☞ Will the school help you find work after graduation?

Interview with a Professional:
Q&A

Mike Nelson

Web design assistant, Scripps Networks Interactive,
Knoxville, Tennessee

Q: *How did you get started?*

A: A local company recruited me through my community college. I also participated in an internship, which provided valuable experience and an immediate opportunity to apply the skills I learned. The internship Web site project went on my résumé, and I created an online portfolio demonstrating examples of my works.

Q: *What's a typical day like?*

A: On a typical day, I process content for several Web sites and publish the content to the server. I use video and image-capture software, digital image editing software (Adobe Photoshop), Flash, FTP, Dreamweaver, and Vignette Content Management. Specific Web technologies include XHTML, CSS [Cascading Style Sheets], [Sun Microsystems] JavaScript, and server configuration. I'm involved with design and development, as well as ongoing Webmaster-type responsibilities.

Q: *What's your advice for those starting a career?*

A: Learn about Web project management and development cycles and methodology. It will provide a high-level view of multiple functions involved in Web site projects of varying scale and scope. Depending on the degree of complexity, a Webmaster may only maintain an existing Web site with few responsibilities outside of maintenance. The difference between Web designer and Webmaster can be significant, or all functions could be combined into one role (Webmaster or Web site manager). At a small company, or if you work for yourself, you may need to wear many hats including graphic/art and print designer, copy editor/researcher, applications programmer, database administrator, Web server administrator, Web language author, marketer, and Web project manager. Whereas a large company typically looks for very sharp specialists in one discipline.

Q: *What's the best part of being a Webmaster?*

A: I like the variety of technologies, skills, business aspects, and people involved in Web technology. The continued advancement, standardization, and refinement of the elements of site design and development are exciting. It keeps my skills sharp and keeps me on my toes. There's never a dull moment.

The Future

The number of Webmasters needed is expected to grow much faster than the average for all occupations between through 2014. That's because more companies are doing more business on the Internet. Companies need these professionals to help make it easier to share information across computers. New technologies, such as wireless networks, will also lead to more jobs. There will be excellent opportunities for people with the latest skills.

Did You Know?

The World Wide Web was invented by Tim Berners-Lee and Robert Cailliau in 1990.

Job Seeking Tips

See the suggestions below and refer to Appendix A for advice on résumés and interviewing.

✔ Perform a simulated job search before you pick your courses.

✔ Design your own site (and be sure to post your résumé on it!).

✔ Evaluate the sites of prospective employers so you understand their purpose and can make constructive suggestions.

✔ Be sure you know the latest software and buzz words.

Career Connections

For more on careers in Web design and administration, contact the following organizations.

World Organization of Webmasters http://www.webprofessionals.org

American Association of Webmasters http://www.aawebmasters.com

Web Design and Developers Association http://www.wdda.org

International Association of Webmasters and Designers http://www.iawmd.com

Associate's Degree Programs

Here are a few two-year schools offering quality Web design and administration programs:

Kishwaukee Community College, Malta, Illinois

Pellissippi State Community College, Knoxville, Tennessee

Queensborough Community College, Queens, New York

Bellevue Community College, Bellevue, Washington

Financial Aid

Here are a few scholarships related to Web design and administration. For more on financial aid for two-year students, turn to Appendix B.

IEEE Computer Society International Design Competition This contest awards $10,000 for Web sites designed to implement computer-based solutions to real-world problems.   http://computer.org/csidc.org

National Science Foundation Scholarships in Science, Technology, Engineering, and Mathematics These scholarships support academically talented, financially needy students, enabling them to enter the workforce following completion of an associate, baccalaureate, or graduate level degree in science and engineering disciplines. http://www.nsf.gov

The World Organization of Webmasters Scholarships (WOW) WOW offers educational opportunities for Web educators and trainers. http://www.webprofessionals.org/articulation/scholar.html

Related Careers

Computer systems analysts, Web and multimedia designers, computer and network operators, Web technicians, computer hardware engineers, computer programmers and developers, database analysts and administrators, graphic designers and illustrators, information systems analysts and consultants, software engineers, systems testing technicians, and user support technicians.

Network/
Systems
Administrator

Vital Statistics

Salary: The median annual salary for network and computer systems administrators is about $58,000, according to 2006 data from the U.S. Bureau of Labor Statistics. Jobs that provide the experience to become a network or systems administrator can pay half that amount.

Employment: This field is expected to continue growing rapidly through 2014, or about twice as fast as all other occupations.

Education: Courses in the design, installation, and improvement of computer networks and related software. A two-year degree can provide entry-level training and coursework needed.

Work Environment: Network and systems administrators normally work in well-lighted, comfortable offices or computer rooms.

Whether you use your computer to research term papers or just enjoy the games you play, you probably know what a difference more memory makes. To get the maximum amount of power from their computers, businesses and other professional organizations now depend on networking their computers so that they can expand their capacity by sharing data and applications. And as they expand their computer networks, corporations are very concerned about security—protecting their information and services.

This means that firms need people who can install, manage, and secure their networks. Network and systems administrators design and support an organization's local area network (LAN), wide area network (WAN), network segment, Internet, and intranet systems. The job can require some real hands-on skills as these professionals may install routers, switches, and system connections. Pros in this field often are well-versed in the nuts and bolts of computers, including motherboards, storage devices, power supplies, ports, and memories. In-depth computer knowledge is key to ensure that networks are up to speed and meeting the daily needs of users.

If you decide to become a network administrator, you'll also be expected to gather data about user needs. Then you will assess your findings in order to identify, interpret, and evaluate system and network requirements. You will design, set up, and maintain your organization's networks, train staff, provide technical support, monitor file use, make sure security is appropriate, and plan and implement changes. The job puts a heavy emphasis on helping all types of computer users, so you'll be interacting constantly with fellow employees, and possibly customers, answering questions and giving helpful advice.

You should also be prepared to provide day-to-day on-site administrative support for users in a variety of work environments, including professional offices, small businesses, government, educational institutions, and large corporations. Employers of computer support specialists and systems administrators range from start-up companies to established industry leaders. Although the range of industries is wide, about 23 percent of all computer network administrators are employed in professional, scientific, and technical services industries, principally computer systems design and related services. Other organizations that employ substantial numbers of network administrators include administrative and support services companies, banks, government agencies, insurance companies, educational institutions, and wholesale and retail vendors of computers, office equipment, appliances, and home electronic equipment. Some network administrators work as consultants for a number of smaller clients.

On the Job

As a network administrator, you'll be working in some kind of office setting but not necessarily at a desk. This job is more "wired" than most, and you may find yourself getting into some tight spots too as you try to make the proper connections under desks.

Depending on the needs of your organization, you may be based at one location or travel among several sites. Those who work as consultants are away from their offices much of the time, sometimes spending months working at a client site. Conversely, if you're managing a large system you may be able to connect to your customer's computers remotely, using modems, laptops, e-mail, and the Internet, to provide technical support to users. This capability can reduce or even eliminate the need for travel.

Network administrators normally work 37 to 40 hours a week, Monday to Friday, but you may need to work overtime when installing systems or if you're on call for breakdowns. You may also be on call for rotating evening or weekend shifts if your firm requires 24/7 support.

Keys to Success

To be a successful network/systems administrator, you need

- excellence at technical activities
- talent to collate complex data
- problem-solving skills
- interest in the field
- superior knowledge of existing hardware and software

- ⚷ a logical, analytical approach
- ⚷ strong communication skills
- ⚷ good team-playing ability
- ⚷ ability to direct and oversee the work of others

A Typical Day at Work

As a network or systems administrator, the size and type of organization largely influence your role where you work. In a vast financial institution, you may have the specific responsibility for one area of a computer system; for a small start-up, you may be the troubleshooter for almost any IT-related problem.

There are, however, many common tasks in this type of work. Here's what a network administrator in a midsized firm may do in the course of a normal day. You start the morning by reviewing any "tickets" (requests for help or notes about problems) that came in the previous day. You may meet with the technicians who fixed the problems to see if there is any pattern indicating a weakness in the system. If you decide there's a problem with the hardware, you check the budget to see if you have the funding to order a replacement for a malfunctioning part. If you think it's the network design that's causing difficulties, you assign one of the team members to come up with a recommendation to change it. If you have staff working on other aspects of the network, you check in with them. Later in the day, you are on a conference call with senior management regarding a new software application they plan to install system-wide. Management wants your expertise regarding the capabilities of that system. You tell them what modifications will have to be made in the application before it will work on your network.

Do You Have What It Takes?

In network administration, you spend a great deal of time solving puzzles and working closely with staff at all levels. Successful administrators have the ability to zero in on problems and intently hammer away at them until they are solved. Since computers are often a business's lifeblood, the job demands that you work at a fast pace. Any computer experience is useful, especially if you have been on the user end of IT (information technolgy) systems, gaining an idea of the problems that arise. Nearly 50 percent of graduates entering this work hold some degree in computer science. Team playing is also valued, whether you've gained that experience through a school organization, part-time job, or other situation.

And, although your studies may focus on communication among computers, communication with people is as important. Potential candidates must explain operations to coworkers who may have no technological smarts. Administrators must keep calm in a crisis and think clearly when trouble rears its head.

> **"Efforts to protect critical computer networks have unfortunately not kept pace with the march of technology."**
> —Jon Kyl, U.S. senator from Arizona

Two-Year Training

While graduates of any discipline with the right background can break into this field, those who study computer networks and telecommunications are strongly preferred. An associate's degree in computer network administration can be earned at many community colleges and trade or technical schools. These programs cover the design, installation, and improvement of computer networks and related software. Coursework may include computer maintenance, network cabling, databases, Windows OS, Unix OS, Cisco networking, and network security. Some two-year programs prepare you for industry-recognized certifications in areas such as CompTIA A+ Certification, MCP or Microsoft Certified Professional, and Cisco Certified Network Associate (CCNA). Other degree programs that can lead to a career in network administration are computer science, electrical/electronic engineering, physics, mathematics, and software engineering.

What to Look For in a School

When considering a two-year school, be sure to ask these questions:

☞ Does the program focus more on preparing students for further education or for the workforce?

☞ Will the program help you prepare for certification exams?

☞ Are instructors certified and actively working in the field?

☞ Does the program have state-of-the-art classrooms and computer labs?

☞ Are hands-on learning activities a regular part of the education?

☞ Does the program coordinate with local companies and organizations to provide internships?

☞ Where are recent graduates working now?

Interview with a Professional:
Q&A

Jeanette Smith

Network Administrator, Sound Inpatient Physicians,
Tacoma, Washington

Q: *How did you get started?*

A: I was really interested in electronics and was introduced as a child to electronics by my grandfather. I would watch him design devices in his basement shop. At the time our automatic garage door required a key to open it. This meant my grandmother had to get out of the car. I watched him design a sending unit and receiving unit from a transistor radio to automatically open the garage door with the push of a button from inside the car. I was truly inspired by his inventiveness.

I was first introduced to the computer industry when I was in my junior high school. I was programming in Basic on a Teletype, which connected to the regional school system mainframe. I was convinced that either electronic engineering or computer sciences was going to be my career choice.

I attended Washington State University for a year but could not continue due to a lack of funds. I returned to California and took a job doing electronic assembling for photovoltaic medical equipment. Later that year I was hired by a systems development company who provided third party computer systems support for the Minuteman and MX Missile telemetry systems...Being a woman in this field is a challenge.

Q: *What's a typical day like?*

A: I first check the backups to assure they have completed. If the backups have not completed then I search the logs to find out why the failure occurred and restart the backup process. I walk through the facility to check on equipment to see that all is working as expected. This is also a good time to be visible and generate a feeling of client satisfaction. Too often technical people avoid the interaction with the office staff and hide with their equipment in the server room. This may have been appropriate behavior in the past, but it is not good practice today. Today, it is necessary to cultivate an interactive relationship with your clients and coworkers. IT staff are now much more visible and integrated into business culture.

In a nutshell, I select, order, and configure equipment and integrate it into the network as needed. I track the software and equipment inventories for the organization. I act as a resource for executive management to determine the best course of action for development of the corporate IT infrastructure into the future. I document all these activities.

I carry a cell phone 24-7. If there is a problem with the network then I am required to respond. I come into the office after hours to apply patches and updates to the servers. If there is a change to the network that will require the interruption of access for the clients then I will perform these tasks after hours.

Q: *What's your advice for those starting a career?*

A: A degree is a necessity to progress in this career field. Eventually, you will hit a wall or be turned down for an opportunity if you lack a degree. Take advantage of internship opportunities while attending college. These opportunities evaporate after you graduate so grab the opportunity to gain experience while gaining a formal education. Certifications are a means of getting noticed or even as a basic requirement for many IT positions. I suggest pursuing certifications in addition to a degree.

Remember that it is communicators and customer service–savvy individuals who will excel in IT careers in the future. Yes, we must continue to develop our technical skills. However, it is the business client we are serving. Know your business and know your clients.

Q: *What's the best part of being a network administrator?*

A: Okay, so I'm a geek! I love to be immersed in the technology.

The Future

Rapid job growth is projected through 2014, according to the Bureau of Labor Statistics. Employment of systems administrators is expected to increase much faster than the average for all occupations as firms continue to rely on speedy computer systems and invest heavily in securing computer networks. Hospitals, financial institutions, technology companies, and retailers all need network administrators, and major corporations have been hiring, such as Kaiser Permanente, Helitek, Franklin First Financial Corporation, Schlumberger, Sony Electronics, SalesLink, Ascent Logic Corporation, Axis Technology, West Valley Technology, and Cotelligen. Expert administrators can advance to become network engineers and network architects.

Job Seeking Tips

Read the suggestions below and turn to Appendix A for advice on résumés and interviewing.

✔ Intern for an Internet service provider (ISP), assisting with technical maintenance.

✔ Volunteer to assist a network administrator.

✔ Research industries that employ network/systems administrators.

✔ Post your résumé on Internet employment sites.

✔ Find out all you can about the jobs and companies for which you interview.

Did You Know?

Data was first transmitted between individual computers more than 50 years ago when scientists at the Massachusetts Institute of Technology (MIT) set up a network for monitoring the air defense of the United States.

Career Connections

For more on careers in network and systems administration, contact the following organizations.

Network and Systems Professionals Association
http://www.naspa.com

USENIX, the Advanced Computing Systems Association
http://www.usenix.org/about

Computer Network Professionals Association http://nui.net/cnpa/

Association of Support Professionals http://www.asponline.com

Computer Technology Industry Association http://www.comptia.org

Associate's Degree Programs

Here are a few two-year schools offering quality network and systems administration programs:

Community College of Allegheny County, Pittsburgh, Pennsylvania

Community College of Vermont, Montpelier, Vermont

Hawkeye Community College, Waterloo, Iowa

Mesa Community College, Mesa, Arizona

Tacoma Community College, Tacoma, Washington

Devry University, various locations

Heald College, various locations

Financial Aid

Here are a few scholarships related to network and systems administration. For more on financial aid for two-year students, turn to Appendix B.

NASPA Foundation Scholarships These awards were established to fund the education, training, and advancement of tomorrow's technical workforce and assist in the retraining and professional development of mid-career professionals. Award amounts vary. http://www.naspa.org/foundation/grants.cfm

The Betty Stevens-Frecknall Scholarship This annual national scholarship supports students seeking an education in an accredited degree program related to information technology.   http://www.edfoundation.org/bettystevensfrecknallscholarship.htm

The Datatel Scholars Foundation Scholarships These funds go to students enrolled in a school that uses Datatel products. Awards range from $1,000 to $2,500.   http://www.datatel.com/global/scholarships

Related Careers

Programmers, software engineers, systems analysts, database administrator, technical support, hardware engineers, information systems analysts, information systems managers, and testing technicians.

Multimedia Specialist

Vital Statistics

Salary: The median annual salary for multimedia specialists is $43,000, according to 2006 figures from the U.S. Bureau of Labor Statistics.

Employment: Multimedia is one of eight computer career clusters that is most in demand in the United States, according to the Information Technology Association of America.

Education: The training needed to work in this field includes the basics of computer programming, graphic design, and audio and video production.

Work Environment: An office or studio outfitted with current digital editing equipment and state of the art computers.

Do you love playing the computer games Battlefield or Flight Simulator? Or maybe you enjoy clicking onto the Comedy Central or MTV Web sites for video clips, sound bytes, and fun self-quizzes. If you're a regular Web wanderer or game fanatic, you know how entertaining multimedia can be. Multimedia brings together combinations of text, audio, graphics, animation, and video to entertain, inform, sell, and educate. The results can dazzle the senses. Often a key component is interactivity—meaning that the Internet sites, computer games, and more will respond to the user's input.

Multimedia is continually integrated into all aspects of our communications. Just look at the latest cell phones that let you watch videos, play music, access the Web, and play games. And you can still use these phones to make calls if you like! Multimedia is also used for corporate Web sites, electronic reference materials, CD-ROM games, ATMs and kiosks, technical training programs, and trade show displays.

As the techno-wizards who combine artistic sense and technical knowledge, multimedia specialists build what are called information and communication technology (ICT)–based products. Opportunities abound for these experts who can weave together sound clips, graphics, photography, video montages, and animation into lively presentations. As the name multimedia suggests, the career requires expertise in several areas:

- Conceptual design—the vision for the overall plan of a game, Web site, or other multimedia project.
- Graphic design—knowledge of the basic art concepts and practices for the design of graphic solutions for visual problems.
- Computer graphics—mastery of software applications such as Photoshop, Illustrator, and Flash that enable computer animation and other visuals.

- Audio design, recording, and editing—skills to record and edit sound files and soundtracks for multimedia productions.
- Video recording and editing—familiarity with programs such as Final Cut Pro, Premier, and Avid to create and edit motion graphics and video footage.
- Writing—the ability to convey ideas, write scripts, and deliver information in a clear and logical way.
- Interactive interface design—facility in using programs to build the interactive elements of a multimedia project.
- Web page design and editing—knowledge of applications such as Dreamweaver and Front Page to design Internet pages.
- Programming—a rudimentary understanding of design problems and program solutions.
- Database design and maintenance—familiarity with database structures.
- Project management—organizational skills to complete a project on time and on budget.

As a multimedia specialist, you'll probably specialize either in interactive or noninteractive media. Multimedia products that are interactive are designed to be played in kiosks on interactive CDs or DVDs, and on some Web sites. They let users navigate to the content they choose to access. As an interactive specialist, your job will be to make sure that all media elements link together effectively and that users can easily find the information they want through a well-designed graphical user interface (GUI, pronounced in "gooey" in the computer world). The GUI is basically the screen design through which the user enters information. Microsoft Windows, for example, is a GUI.

With noninteractive multimedia, navigation is not possible. Noninteractive multimedia take the form of TV commercials, Web sites using Flash intros, or movies. Some business presentations are also built using programs such as Adobe Premiere, Macromedia Director, Adobe Photoshop, and Microsoft Office Suite's PowerPoint.

As a multimedia specialist, you'll likely work at a firm that specializes in media production. These firms usually hire a few full-time designers and numerous freelance designers who have skills related to specific projects. Among the projects you'll work on are the development of DVD, CD-ROM, Web, and video material. People with multimedia skills also work for television stations, Internet service providers, graphic art services, and other media outlets. If you are trained in and have knowledge of instructional design and media communications, you might work for a school district or a college. Of course, the game design industry especially craves enthusiastic multimedia specialists to churn out action-packed entertainment combining programming, 3-D design, and animation.

Finally, some multimedia specialists are self-employed and work on a contract basis with a variety of clients ranging from nonprofits to business and government.

On the Job

The majority of multimedia designers work in an office or studio, although many travel to meet clients on-site. Dress is usually business casual because these professionals mostly toil away from public view, behind their computer screens. As a multimedia designer, you usually work from 9:00 a.m. to 5:00 p.m., although this career often offers flexible work schedules, sometimes part-time or from home, or both. Keep in mind that many multimedia jobs have tight deadlines, so you may be expected to work late or on weekends to finish a project on time. While most hours are spent on your own bringing together the media elements required of a project, you will have to collaborate with coworkers who are specialists in their fields. Video directors, music producers, and animators may give you their work, which you will integrate in the final project.

> "An iPod, a phone, an Internet mobile communicator... these are *not* three separate devices."
> —Steve Jobs, president of Apple Inc., introducing the new iPhone

Keys to Success

To be a successful multimedia specialist, you need:

- creativity, curiosity, and imagination
- strong computer skills, including a knowledge of software and programming languages
- drawing skills
- superior communication and presentation skills
- an understanding of the best media to reach different audiences
- excellent organization and time-management
- drive to meet deadlines
- good team playing
- ability to take criticism
- interest in new technological developments

Do You Have What It Takes?

People who work in this relatively new field say it's exciting, demanding, and the ideal choice if you're a creative person who embraces technology. While ideal candidates have design and artistic sense, they also know how to apply these talents to make products that are user friendly. Although you don't necessarily need high-level programming skills, some programming know-how certainly helps, and you'll need to understand how technologies are integrated. If you learn the different aspects of computer design, including coding, databases, and networking, you will be able to make well-informed decisions. You need to be able to see "the big picture" and have a sense of how your designs will appear and be used. It pays to have a grasp of the various platforms on which multimedia projects now appear, including PCs, gaming devices, iPods, televisions, and cell phones. Good communicators excel in this field as it requires an ability to express ideas verbally and visually. Also, this industry wants sticklers for detail—there is very little room for error in multimedia production. And you must enjoy working on your own as well as in a team.

A Typical Day at Work

As a multimedia specialist, your day depends on your current project. After arriving at your studio, you'll probably check e-mail messages from account managers and clients. If there's any information that affects a project in progress, you may interrupt the flow of your work to tackle any crisis, large or small. If a concept you've helped develop has been approved, you might spend your day working up the basic design and considering which elements should be incorporated—video, audio, animation, etc. These elements may require the collaboration of other specialists—writers, animators and programmers. Or you might meet with clients to discuss a proposal, make recommendations, or start developing some initial ideas for approval. Your role at meetings will be to advise on design issues. You'll be expected to interpret what the client wants in design terms and decide how it can best be achieved within budget. As a project nears completion, you may test it with a focus group and make adjustments according to their reactions and results. When a project you've worked on is complete, you may have to field questions from the press. In an entry-level job, you may also spend a lot of time authoring files; using hypertext markup language (HTML) or "object-oriented" programming languages such as Java or C++, testing and adjusting final programs, or producing product documentation.

How to Break In

Because no set standards for this profession are established, titles can vary. One element of your job search will involve determining which positions really require an expertise in blending various media. If you graduate with a multimedia degree, investigate positions such as scriptwriter, Web designer, producer, training designer, and Web editor, which all require multimedia talents. Well-established multimedia educational programs are limited but can certainly connect you to internships and entry-level job opportunities. Landing a position may come about on the basis of projects you've created with Photoshop, Flash, and other technologies. These projects don't have to be samples from a previous job; they can be multimedia works you've produced on your own. An impressive portfolio demonstrates that you can use your imagination, integrate media and technology, and work on schedule and within a budget.

Two-Year Training

Although the number of schools that offer a major in this field is small, it is growing. What's more, many institutions allow you to major in computer technologies and then supplement your program with courses in multimedia design. Students of digital communications and multimedia learn the technical, creative, and business skills necessary to design, develop, market, and manage digital media. A solid two-year education highlights digital animation, e-commerce, information design, information law and ethics, introduction to digital design, introduction to multimedia, programming for digital media, two- and three-dimensional design, and Web site management. Students should learn the basics of computer programming, graphic design, and audio and video production, and then apply that knowledge to generate computer animation, build Web sites, and produce CD-ROMs and DVDs. The business end should not go neglected. Multimedia students benefit from courses in marketing, law, and distribution. It's a lot to learn, but multimedia specialists are in such great demand that those late nights in the computer lab should definitely pay off.

What to Look For in a School

When considering a two-year school, be sure to ask these questions:

- ☞ Does the program offer a concentration in your area of interest, such as design, e-commerce, or writing for digital media?
- ☞ Does it have a reputation in that field?
- ☞ Does the program focus more on design or on technical skills?
- ☞ Are the labs up-to-date with the most current software?

☞ Will you have the chance to create a senior project?

☞ Will the department help you find work after graduation?

☞ What are recent grads doing now?

Interview with a Professional:
Q&A
Preston Northrup
Film/video editor, Remote Control Monkey, Hollywood, California

Q: *How did you get started?*

A: I liked the lifestyle of people I knew that edited film, but I knew I wasn't going to get anywhere unless I knew what I was doing. So I took some classes and met some people who were working already. I developed relationships with people as well as my skills in editing, and before I knew it, I was lead editor on a skateboarding show.

Q: *What's a typical day like?*

A: The best part about a fast-paced job like a TV editor is that no day is typical. To put it simply, I go to work and sit in front of the computer for 6–15 hours, and then I go home. But time spent in front of that screen going through hours of footage is never boring. There's always a new or different way of doing things, and the possibilities are endless.

Q: *What's your advice for those starting a career?*

A: My advice is to learn as much as you can while it's free or cheap. Find people who are doing what you want to do and make sure it's what you really want to do.

Q: *What's the best part of being a multimedia specialist?*

A: The best part of this job is deciding what is good and what isn't. To see your ideas presented to millions, whether they realize it or not. And the fact that you're making something great that could just be okay.

The Future

Since the popularity of digital media keeps increasing, career opportunities seem unlimited. Indeed, the Information Technology Association of America (ITAA) has reported that multimedia specialist is one of the eight computer career clusters that is most in demand. Two factors are helping spur job growth in this area: The cost of multimedia software and hardware is falling, and outlets for multimedia communications are expanding from the Internet to cell phones to iPods and beyond.

Did You Know?

The term *multimedia* was coined in 1965 to describe events like the Exploding Plastic Inevitable, organized by the artist Andy Warhol. These events combined live rock music, film, experimental lighting, and performance art.

Job Seeking Tips

See the suggestions below and turn to Appendix A for advice on résumés and interviewing.

- ✔ Network or get to know people who are connected to what you want to do.
- ✔ Get your reel or multimedia portfolio together to show employers what you're capable of.
- ✔ Don't stop learning, even after you're finished with school.
- ✔ Research firms that interest you.
- ✔ Be ready to explain how you can be an asset to a potential employer.

Career Connections

For more on careers in multimedia, contact the following organizations.

Society for Technical Communications http://www.stc.org

Information Technology Association of America http://www.itaa.org

Association for Multimedia Communications http://www.amcomm.org

Associate's Degree Programs

Here are a few two-year schools offering quality multimedia programs:

Bristol Community College, Fall River, Massachusetts

Delaware County Community College, Media, Pennsylvania

Fulton-Montgomery Community College, Johnstown, New York

Los Angeles Mission College, Los Angeles, California

Portland Community College, Portland, Oregon
Raritan Valley Community College, Somerville, New Jersey
Tacoma Community College, Tacoma, Washington

Financial Aid

Here are a couple scholarships related to multimedia. For more on financial aid for two-year students, turn to Appendix B.

StraightForward Media This organization does all its charitable giving exclusively through college scholarships, including media and communications scholarships in the amount of $500 per student. http://www.straightforwardmedia.com

Society for Technical Communications This group awards scholarships to students enrolled in technical communication programs at universities, colleges, junior colleges, and technical schools. http://www.stc.org

Related Careers

Advertising, marketing, and public relations managers; art directors; graphic designers; public relations specialists; and Web designers.

Cybersecurity
Expert

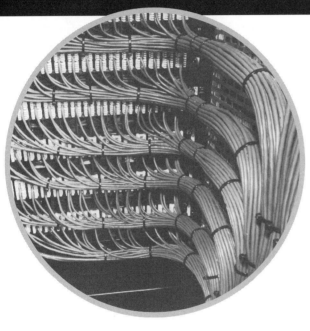

Vital Statistics

Salary: Computer specialists working in areas of cybersecurity earn a median annual salary of $42,750, according to 2006 figures from the U.S. Bureau of Labor Statistics.

Employment: Employment for cybersecurity experts will be strong in every field, increasing faster than average and much faster than average, respectively, for support specialists and systems administrators relative to all other occupations through 2014. Also, in the field of computer programming—whose growth will slacken due to outsourcing—professionals with knowledge of digital technology security issues will be sought-after.

Education: An associate's degree in information security, cybersecurity management, computer science, or a related field, plus certification in a particular application.

Work Environment: Security specialists work at terminals in offices and computer labs.

While most of us fear the possibility of contracting a computer virus or having our identities stolen online, there's one type of computer user who sees these possibilities, not as threats, but as challenges—even opportunities. These professionals are trained in cybersecurity (also called *information security*).

Not long ago, businesses took care of all their security concerns with a front-desk guard and an alarm system. But because today computers hold some corporations' most valuable assets, cyber crime has spread, and the specialized field of cybersecurity has expanded rapidly. These professionals protect data from unauthorized users, and they work under titles such as data security analyst, data security supervisor, and Web security administrator. Specialized steganographers also work in this field. They study computer files to see if they contain any hidden messages.

All these professionals have a full understanding of the programs and passwords that are used to limit access to data. Most must be familiar with firewalls. These are information technology security devices that permit or deny connections to a computer. Firewalls are also called border protection devices (BPDs). Firewalls are commonly used if you have an Internet connection. They help protect your computer from viruses that can destroy data or from hackers—cyber thieves who want to steal credit card numbers, bank account information, and other valuable data. Hackers who can capture your personal data can use your credit card number and rack up huge purchases made in your name. Imagine the shock of getting a credit card bill showing thousands of dollars in purchases that you did not make.

The types of industries that are most concerned with securing data are banking and finance; chemical; oil and gas; transportation; water supply systems; law enforcement; health care; and defense. Protecting these vital information structures is a high priority nowadays. There's even concern over cyber terrorists who could use their technological know-how to shut down power grids, disable communication systems, and halt the delivery of medical supplies.

Whatever your title, you'll be responsible for tracking and preventing viruses, detecting hackers, and recovering information from technology disasters. You'll be expected to monitor networks for security breaches, design and implement the security applications of e-commerce programs, install security software, and collect data for use in the prosecution of cyber crimes. In addition, you may initiate education campaigns to teach users the importance of computer security.

Information security is a career for people who like to learn something every day. The field is always in flux, and new products come out regularly to thwart those who want to exploit the vulnerabilities in the latest software. As a security professional, you'll have to rely heavily on books, seminars, and Web sites to keep up-to-date in your efforts to catch cyber crooks.

Above all, you can expect it to be challenging, rewarding, and strategic. After all, you're being asked to help protect the vital assets of your organization. If you keep data safe, you're an invaluable asset to your firm.

Keys to Success

To be a successful cybersecurity expert, you need
- strong mathematical ability
- a precise approach
- to be a logical thinker who is good at abstractions
- imagination and creativity
- good team-playing ability
- problem-solving skills
- customer service skills

On the Job

Like most IT technicians, cybersecurity specialists work in well-lighted, comfortable offices or labs. You'll usually work about 40 hours a week, but you'll probably be "on call" via Blackberry or cell phone and expected to put in overtime if there's an emergency. Cybersecurity experts report on security vulnerabilities and often work closely with software developers to build protective systems. As a cyber pro, you often meet with top management to understand what information requires protection and discuss solutions: passwords, antivirus software, firewalls, and computer locks. Purchasing and installing systems are part of your regular duties and you may help back up data as well. Regular backup is an important safety measure—if a computer virus destroys data, a company will be relieved to have essential information stored elsewhere.

Do You Have What It Takes?

It actually helps in this field if you can think like a criminal. So along with having a passion for computer software, systems, and programming, you need to use logic to outsmart and thwart cyber criminals. You'll need to have the psychological savvy to intuit how hackers and other cyber criminals think and the technical skills to understand how their actions could impact a computer system. An interest in criminal justice is certainly a plus. "So much of what's involved in defending (computer) systems involves how to creatively put the pieces together the right way," remarks one expert.

A Typical Day at Work

In the workaday world of cybersecurity, you start by making sure that no workers are experiencing security problems. If there is a report of a security breach, you have to get the details down and address the problem immediately. Although you may have an agenda for the week, each day's schedule needs to be adjusted as new jobs pop up on short notice.

Assuming no emergencies arise, you might start your day by reviewing the latest patches provided by your antivirus program and arranging for their installation on the company's network. If all goes well, you can get this done before you're due at a meeting of the company's security analysis team. The meeting is about a security-review report that you're helping write. You provide a brief summary of what your research has turned up so far and make notes on additional follow-up that's needed.

After lunch, you tackle a list of possible problems. This requires several hours of calls and e-mails to find out if the fixes you've installed are working and whether additional actions will be required. Toward the end of the day, you log into some online chats or call colleagues to get their take on some of the hot issues affecting the security business.

How to Break In

While there's been a slowdown in hiring for the information technology sector recently, it has not affected opportunities for security specialists. To be competitive in this job market, it's essential to master the fundamentals.

This means practicing everything you study until you have it down cold. It's especially helpful to set up a network at home and equip it with firewalls, passwords, and other protective measures. You might also volunteer to help a local nonprofit, like your local YMCA, to set up and secure a computer network. This type of work can give you the invaluable skills and references to secure a career-track job later on. Try to gain server and network-engineering experience especially.

Certification can open doors and many associate's degree programs in security management are designed to prep their students for these exams. Software companies may have their own certification programs to handle their protection issues—check with major software firms to find out about their specific training requirements. You can also learn security procedures and techniques on the job by taking an entry-level position as a desk technician network administrator or telecommunications technician.

> ## "Treat your password like your toothbrush. Don't let anybody else use it, and get a new one every six months"
> —Clifford Stoll, author of *The Cuckoo's Egg: Tracking a Spy Through the Maze of Computer Espionage*

What to Look For in a School

When considering a two-year school, be sure to ask these questions:

☞ What certifications do the faculty have?

☞ Does the coursework cover the latest software and other technology?

☞ Will you be able to specialize in fields such as artificial intelligence or database management?

☞ What is the employment history of recent graduates?

☞ Are there internship opportunities that provide hands-on experience?

Two-Year Training

Associate's degrees in cybersecurity are booming and they combine a unique blend of coursework. Typical classes include introduction to business, security management, business communications, criminal justice, psychology, policing, private security, and criminal law. Plus, training covers computer science basics and related material, including information systems, engineering, math, and physics. You will learn about the needs of computer and network systems, as well as about devices and procedures such as cryptography, which is coding used to protect computers. Within the security training, there are specialties. For example, a two-year degree in computer forensics, which teaches how to sift through data, even deleted e-mails, to find evidence of wrongdoing.

The Future

The Bureau of Labor Statistics reports that cybersecurity will be a $20 billion industry within the next few years. As a result, the projected growth in the number of cybersecurity professionals will have an annual compounded rate of nearly 14 percent from 2006 through at least 2008, according to a study released by IDC, a market intelligence provider. As threats of terrorism continue, more professionals will be hired to address national security matters as well.

> **"The only truly secure system is one that is powered off, cast in a block of concrete, and sealed in a lead-lined room with armed guards."**
> —Gene Spafford, computer security expert

Did You Know?

In a recent FBI survey, 90 percent of companies said they'd had a computer security breach.

Job Seeking Tips

See the suggestions below and turn to Appendix A for advice on résumés and interviewing.

✔ Since government agencies have a major stake in keeping our networks secure, check for jobs on the Web sites of national and international agencies, as well as more traditional corporate and academic sites.

✔ Because this is an especially dynamic part of the technology industry, be sure you're up-to-date on the latest software and patches.

✔ Check out which recruiters specialize in this area.

✔ Attend conferences—especially ones that offer "hands-on" training—to meet and create new contacts.

Interview with a Professional:
Q&A

Richard Campbell

Network security architect, The Cobalt Group,
Seattle, Washington

Q: *How did you get started?*

A: As a high school senior I actually flunked my first computer class. I said at the time I would never touch another computer unless you could talk to it. Then in 1996, a friend asked if I had seen something or other on the Internet. I asked him what the Internet was. I went over to his house to see what all the buzz was about, and I was immediately hooked. By 1997 I had bought my first computer and read every single book I could get my hands on, particularly anything that had to do with security and hacking systems. I knew I wanted to get some "formal" training, so I researched all the schools in my area. My local community college consistently was rated as one of the best, due to its ties to the local IT industry leaders, who helped drive the course curriculum and industry needs.

I knew, from the time I started school, I wanted to be in security. When it came to looking for work, I was completely focused and near obsessed with getting the type of job I wanted. My first computing job was as an intern for Boeing working in the Site Operations department. That basically meant I went out to help fix people's computer and network problems when the help desk wasn't able to help via the phone. I never dreamed I would get to work for Boeing full time, but I did everything I could to create my own opportunities. During that nine-month internship, I went around to any manager that had the word *security* in their title. Out of 175 interns that went into Boeing's intern program, I was one of three who made it to a "real" Boeing job.

I was then hired by the Information Protection group. I was to provide technical information related to computer security and data and information protection to the senior manager. Basically, he would ask questions like "How do we protect our pager system from being hacked?" or "How do we protect our data using encryption?"

I moved up to protecting all computing and networking systems, providing vulnerability assessments, threat mitigation, investigations of real or suspected computer crimes, and enforcement of computer use policies. I also helped to create processes and procedures for computer and network assessments. On several incidents, I have worked with the FBI Joint Terror

(continued on next page)

(continued from previous page)

Task Force (JTTF), state and federal attorney generals, and local police departments.

Currently, I work for The Cobalt Group where my title is network security architect. Job duties include not only all the tasks that were described above but redesigning the entire network, in a secured fashion; creating and/or modifying the entire security architecture; and implementing security policies and procedures.

Q: *What's a typical day like?*

A: Like any computer and network security job, it's all about putting out fires. Currently, I *am* the security department, so everything is on me. I'm constantly looking for computer and network weaknesses, keeping up on new and old vulnerabilities, trying to implement security strategies, redesigning the network and attending meetings that relate to information protection or any type of possible security-exploit situations. I'm involved with writing all and any new security computer policies, and the enforcement of those policies. Since I'm also doing the network redesign, I work hand in hand with the network engineer and trying to make sure the business keeps flowing.

Q: *What's your advice for those starting a career?*

A: The problem with the computer security field is that every employer is looking for qualified individuals with a *ton* of experience and background. Unfortunately, there really is no entry-level position for security. So, the only real place to start is by getting as much education and training as one can get, along with server administration or server/network engineering experience. This means starting at the bottom and getting at least three years of hands-on experience.

For my career, I happened to have a law enforcement background, so I was already in the security mode. Plus, I basically taught myself a lot before I went into school and continue to do so now. I made my own opportunities and proved myself to the hiring manager before, during, and after I was hired. I eventually received my master's degree in network security (MSNS). I *always* have a new book, new article, or new information that I'm reading and learning in this field.

Q: *What's the best part of being an information security specialist?*

A: I get to come to work knowing I'm creating a better and safer place for the computers, networks, data, and users. I'm protecting an entire infrastructure from potential and real threats. Usually, when someone is hired into a company, all they are really getting is someone else's mess to take over. I get to actually "redo it"—security the way I want it.

Career Connections

For more on careers in cybersecurity, contact the following organizations.

Association of Computer Support Specialists http://www.acss.org

Association of Support Professionals http://www.asponline.com

System Administrators Guild http://www.sage.org

National Workforce Center for Emerging Technologies http://www.nwcet.org

Cyber Security Industry Alliance https://www.csialliance.org

Colloquium for Information Systems Security Education http://infosecuritymag

Associate's Degree Programs

Here are a few two-year schools offering quality computer programming programs:

Luzerne County Community College, Nanticoke, Pennsylvania

Green River Community College, Auburn, Washington

Morain Valley Community College, Palos Hills, Illinois

Raritan Valley Community College, North Branch, New Jersey

Tulsa Community College, Tulsa, Oklahoma

Northwestern Business College, Naperville, Illinois

Financial Aid

Here are a few scholarships related to cybersecurity. For more on financial aid for two-year students, turn to Appendix B.

Horizons Foundation Scholarship Program The organization Women in Defense sponsors the Horizons Scholarship award to encourage women to pursue careers related to U.S. national security interests. http://wid.ndio.org/horizon

Office of Personnel Management's Scholarships for Service: Cyber Corps The Office of Personnel Management's Cyber Corps program offers up to two years of tuition, room, board, books, and an annual stipend for undergraduates and graduate students at selected colleges and universities who are interested in the "information assurance" field. http://www.sfs.opm.gov

U.S. Department of Homeland Security—Undergraduate Scholarships and Graduate Fellowships Up to 100 awards "intended for students interested in pursuing the basic science and technology innovations that can be applied to the DHS mission." http://www .orau.gov/dhsed

Related Careers

Computer programmers, computer software engineers, computer systems analysts, computer scientists, and database administrators.

Nanoscience Technician

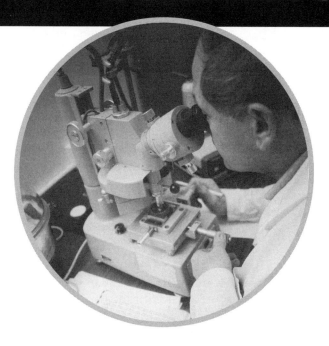

Vital Statistics

Salary: Science technicians have a wide range of earnings, but those working in nanoscience earn at the top in their respective fields, or close to $52,000 a year, according to 2006 figures from the U.S. Bureau of Labor Statistics. Entry-level science technicians earn closer to $30,000 a year.

Employment: Although growth in the number of working science technicians will slightly lag the average for all occupations through 2014, nanoscience technicians will see growing prospects. The National Science Foundation counted 20,000 nanotechnologists worldwide in 2006 and forecasts that the needs of the field will require 2 million workers by 2020.

Education: Nanotechnology bridges many disciplines—chemistry, physics, materials science, engineering, biology, and medicine. Workers who excel in this field should have some educational background in several of these areas.

Work Environment: Comfortable, well-lit offices and labs.

Imagine a medical device that travels through the human body and destroys cancer cells. Or a box as small as a die that contains the entire contents of the Library of Congress. Or materials lighter than steel with 10 times the strength. These are just some of the dreams that inspire the emerging field of nanotechnology.

Nanotechnology is recognized by many as the catalyst for the next major scientific revolution. This new field is expected to create between 800,000 and 2 million new jobs, according to Jack Uldrich and Deb Newberry in their book, *The Next Big Thing Is Really Small*.

Nanotechnology is the advanced, almost futuristic, science of creating electronic devices, microsensors, machines, biomedical equipment, and other products from single atoms and molecules. Matter is manipulated at the molecular level to build longer-lasting, cleaner, safer, and smarter equipment for hospitals, the home, transportation, agriculture, and industry in general.

Although you may not be familiar with the term *nanotechnology*, chances are you've already benefited from it in the form of sunscreen, stain-resistant fabric, antimicrobial bandages, a tennis racket, or even socks. Currently, the main applications for nanotechnology are in building computers, cell phones, laptops, PDAs, digital cameras, and MP3 players.

Nanoparticles are also being integrated in household products including paints, papers, and polymers. In medicine, researchers are developing "nanorobots" that can be programmed to function as antibodies capable of seeking out and destroying viruses and bacteria.

In this field, products are created from microscopic matter measured in terms of nanometers (a nanometer is one billionth of a meter, or 1/80,000th the size of a human hair). Nanomaterials are being used to construct "smart" items like self-tinting automotive glass. One nanomaterial called titanium dioxide absorbs solar energy and converts it into electricity when combined with a specific dye. The hope is to use this nanomaterial to make solar-powered products.

Nanotechnology requires a wide variety of technical skills and knowledge, including electrical engineering, materials science, chemistry, physics, mechanical engineering, and software engineering. The nanotech revolution combines the frontier spirit of Gold Rush days with the mystical quest of alchemy. By controlling the structure of matter at the smallest scale, nanotechnologists may possibly launch a new age in all areas of human endeavor. Auto body technicians and concrete and masonry workers will need to learn to work with new paints and polymer coatings. Color-changing fabrics, embeddable light panels, and stain-resistant furniture will affect architecture and interior design. Doctors will employ nanorobots to destroy cancer cells or perform delicate surgeries. There's even speculation that nanorobots could slow or reverse the aging process. Manufacturing that uses this "bottom-up" method of nanotechnology creates less pollution than conventional manufacturing processes. Environmental issues also could be impacted if nanorobots can be programmed to rebuild the thinning ozone layer and reduce pollutants.

As a career, nanotechnology holds so much potential for growth that techies of all kinds are scrambling to get into it. Currently, most companies working with nanotechnology are in the research stage of development, so research technicians are in great need. Research and production groups working in nanotechnology usually involve specialists from chemistry, engineering, physics, biology, and mathematics.

Research technicians focus on the practical matters of scientific experimentation and research. They support the work of senior scientists and engineers by performing experiments, operating and maintaining equipment such as an atomic force microscope (AFM), and verifying the nanoscale properties of materials. They typically spend their time on pre-production testing and quality assurance procedures associated with new-product development. Or they may carry out inspections and acceptance testing of new product components and subsystems. These responsibilities require them to extensively use computers, computer-interfaced equipment, robotics, and high-technology industrial applications, such as biological engineering. However, some nanoscience technicians work in other areas such as technical sales and marketing.

Employers can be found in many fields, including electronics, aerospace, vacuum technology, optical manufacturing, semiconductor manufacturing, and biotech/agriculture. Some of the companies using nanotechnology are very large and well established, while others in the start-up stage may have less than 50 employees.

On the Job

Nanoscience technicians work mostly in very clean lab-like conditions that can accommodate highly sensitive equipment. Technicians operate state-of-the-art gear such as atomic force microscopes, scanning electron microscopes, vacuum equipment, and plasma reactors. Most have regular hours; however, they occasionally work irregular shifts to monitor experiments that cannot be completed during the regular day. The job requires research, observation, and measurement. Many technicians must carefully record measurements, values, and other results that will be analyzed to develop future products.

> ## "I suspect that when people actually move off the planet they will do it with the awesome powers of nanotechnology."
> ### —Keith Henson, electrical engineer and writer on life extension and cryonics

 ## Keys to Success

To be a successful nanoscience technician, you need
- high mechanical aptitude
- analytical thinking
- interest in most aspects of science
- a background in chemistry, physics, and biology
- an eye for detail and precision
- organizational ability

Do You Have What It Takes?

A career in nanotechnology requires sound analytical abilities, aptitude for basic science, and the ability to handle sophisticated equipment like a sub-atomic microscope, which is needed to explore the nano world. If you have a natural interest in chemistry, physics, and math, this may be a field worth exploring. This career is all about the elements, so you have to know your periodic table. You should also welcome challenges—nanoscience is a very new area and the rules are still being written as to how it all functions. There are frustrations, but the scientific breakthroughs are very rewarding. Since computers assist with research and development, especially for modeling, computer skills are a must. A lot of nanotechnology jobs involve doing research and keeping records, so organizational skills are key. Communication is important as well, because technicians are called on to report their findings both orally and in writing. In addition, advances depend on teamwork, so you'll be expected to work well with others.

A Typical Day at Work

Technicians usually begin as trainees in routine positions under the direct supervision of a scientist or a more experienced technician. As a technician, your team may very well included PhDs in physics and biochemistry. You may even find yourself working in the "clean room" of a nanotechnology institute. Here you may be assisting with the research regarding the development of a product using a new chemical composition. You may be asked to complete an overview of the whole project. This will help you better understand the overall goals of the project. When you report to work each day, your supervisor apprises you of which experiments or tests are being run that day. You're responsible for setting up the equipment and laboratory instruments scientists will be working with that day and making sure they are all in good working order. Technicians perform experiments involving photonics, X-ray defraction, and nanoelectronics, and you may be called upon to operate the equipment yourself. You should be prepared to contribute suggestions and volunteer to run tests.

As the day progresses, you and your colleagues start getting results, which you record for them. Depending on the project, you may have to do calculations based on these figures. As you gain more experience, you'll get a chance to take on more responsibility and carry out assignments under only general supervision.

How to Break In

The first step is to get the right training. Many of those best prepared to enter this field have taken an associate's degree program in nanoscience. However, because nanotechnology is multidisciplinary, some experts recommend studying several different sciences with a focus on the problems associated with nanotechnology, such as developing instrumentation and practical applications.

The more research experience you get in school the better. Starting positions can range from studying original ideas in the lab to carrying out experiments and filling other support roles. In addition to the right mix of studies, it's helpful to do an internship that will give you real-life experience in this sector. Internships can help confirm if a career is right for you. One expert commented that software engineers might not necessarily like nanotech: "Some people in software are good about bits, but they can't think about atoms." So find out for yourself.

Two-Year Training

Since the field of nanotechnology is multidisciplinary in nature, you need as much exposure as possible to three core disciplines: science, engineering, and math. Among the specific courses that will be helpful are materials science, chemistry, biology, physics, electronics, and engineering, with a particular emphasis on atomic and molecular chemistry, solid state physics, and molecular/cellular biology. A growing number of institutions award two-year degrees to become nanoscience technicians. Specific courses include computer simulation, nanoelectronics, nanobiotech, and nanomaterials. Students in practical two-year programs get hands-on training in labs dealing with microfabrication, biochips, or other nano-related materials.

What to Look For in a School

When considering a two-year school, be sure to ask these questions:

☞ Does the school have a multidisciplinary approach?

☞ Are the lab facilities of superior quality?

☞ Does the program feature any corporate partnerships?

☞ What is the school's experience with obtaining National Science Foundation (NSF) grants?

☞ What is the availability of internships associated with the program?

☞ Do professors have a working background in nanotechnology?

The Future

Although the business is in its infancy (like the computer industry was in the 1960s), it is expected to grow enormously. According to the NSF, the total market for nanotech products will reach $1 trillion by 2015, which is equal to about 10 percent of global industrial output in 2006. And job opportunities are booming as nanotech advances affect every sector of industry, including health care, fashion, sports gear, electronics, and aerospace technology.

Interview with a Professional:
Q&A

Thomas L. Olson

Line maintenance technician specialist, Diffusion/
Thin Films (Cypress Semiconductor),
Bloomington, Minnesota

Q: *How did you get started?*

A: Normandale Community College labeled its nanotechnology programs as the "Vacuum Technology Program." The program was conceived by a consortium of manufacturers near the Twin Cities that needed a more specialized worker than what the basic electronics or mechanical engineering programs could provide.

I was a bartender at a local establishment. I already had a two-year associate's degree. A patron of mine was working at Cypress, which manufactures semiconductors. I needed a job with benefits, and he brought me aboard. I started out in the ranks moving the product. It was unlike anything I had ever seen. In the "cleanroom," there is cleaner air than in a hospital operating room. [The work environment has to be particle-free to manufacture semiconductors.] Wow! Robotic arms and computer screens were everywhere. There were vacuum chambers with plasma glow discharges. It was foreign yet highly intriguing. I became very interested in when the equipment had errors or was being dismantled for preventive maintenance. I would give the maintenance personnel as much information as I could about the nature of the error or other equipment problems. I even started feeding them my armchair diagnosis. I asked how I could get into the field, and they said electronics school. Along came the nanotechnology (vacuum) program, and I signed up. Cypress paid for every dime of it. That was going on nine years ago now or so. I worked full time, so it took me a bit longer than two years. But, the demand for the skill was there, so I got a maintenance technician slot well ahead of my official graduation from the program.

Q: *What's a typical day like?*

A: At Cypress here we work 12-hour shifts—alternating three days one week, four days the next. So at any given time we have three to four days off per week. I work 6:00 a.m. to 6:15 p.m. The 15-minute overlap is for "passdown" [a time to explain recurring or new equipment issues]. We use a computer program to track and see priority of work for the wafer fabrication

(continued on next page)

(continued from previous page)

facility. We coordinate with manufacturing management on taking equipment on scheduled downs for preventive maintenance. We meet with engineers to discuss equipment-related issues, plans for equipment upgrades, or new types of spare parts. We create and modify technical documentation on procedures for various equipment sets. We seek out new ways to reduce costs, improve safety, and increase factory output.

Q: *What's the best part of being a science technician?*

A: There is never the same day twice. I believe from what I've heard, it's fairly typical of the industry. I work with a 30-year veteran of the semiconductor industry, and he says that he learns something new every day. Another advantage is the diversity. I work with different departmental disciplines from San Francisco all the way around to Shanghai. There's a lot of interpersonal interaction, and it keeps things interesting.

The work we do also offers instant gratification. When one finds and fixes either solo or in collaboration, it's a good feeling. There's a certain rush with that level of intensity. Jobs are especially rewarding when the equipment is a critical piece that may shut down or hold up an entire production line. It can make a hero in a hurry, or just the opposite.

Q: *What's your advice for those starting a career in nanotechnology?*

A: To be good, you've got to be self-motivated. Take initiative. Seek out ways to improve your skill on your own. The one who takes initiative is the winner, and the most revered among peers. I firmly believe that the program at my school allowed me to know exactly what senior-level technicians were talking about from my very first day. This allowed me to accelerate my ability level rapidly and noticeably, which has led to faster promotions and bigger raises.

Did You Know?

Nanotechnology has been widely depicted in movies and television. Several episodes of the *Jimmy Neutron: Boy Genius* feature nanobots, and in the film *The Hulk*, the Hulk is mutated by nanomeds and nanorobots.

Job Seeking Tips

See the suggestions below and turn to Appendix A for advice on résumés and interviewing.

✔ Get as much hands-on experience as possible.

✔ Attend nanotech conferences.

✔ Read the latest nanotech articles online or in magazines and journals.

✔ Join organizations related to this field; they can be a good source for job leads.

✔ Research companies to find work opportunities that best suit your skills and interests.

Career Connections

For more on careers in nanotechnology, contact the following organizations.

Nanotechnology Institute of the American Society of Mechanical Engineers http://www.nanotechnologyinstitute.org

Nanotechnology Council Virtual Communities of the Institute of Electrical and Electronics Engineers, Inc. http://www.ieee.org

Materials Research Society's Nanotechnology Initiative http://www.mrs.org

Nano Science and Technology Institute http://www.nsti.org

National Nanotechnology Infrastructure Network http://www.nnin.org

Associate's Degree Programs

Here are a few two-year schools offering quality nanoscience technician programs:

Dakota County Technical College, Rosemont, Minnesota

Forsyth Technical Community College, Winston-Salem, North Carolina

Normandale Community College, Bloomington, Minnesota

Edmonds Community College, Lynnwood, Washington

Lock Haven University, Lock Haven, Pennsylvania

Financial Aid

There are very few scholarships directly related to nanotechnology. Some two-year schools offer awards for study in nanoscience, and here are a few programs that may help those interested in the field. For more on financial aid for two-year students, turn to Appendix B.

The **Eugene Borson Scholarship** This award in the amount of $500, is offered annually by the Institute of Environmental Sciences and Technology (IEST) for the best original technical paper(s) written by a student in a topic related to the environmental sciences in connection with controlled environments, particularly through contamination control and nanotechnologies, in which products and equipment are manufactured, processed, or tested.   http://www.iest.org/technical/scholarships/scholarships.html

Intel Science Talent Search for High School Seniors This is America's oldest and most highly regarded pre-college science competition. It provides up to $100,000 in funding.   http://www.intel.com/education/sts

The **Siemens Competition in Math, Science and Technology**   This contest recognizes remarkable talent early on, fostering individual growth for high school students who are willing to challenge themselves through science research. National finalists can win up to $100,000.   http://www.siemens-foundation.org/competition

Related Careers

Engineering technicians, health technologists and technicians, clinical laboratory technologists and technicians, diagnostic medical sonographers, and radiologic technologists and technicians.

Computer Systems Installer

Vital Statistics

Salary: The median annual earnings of computer support specialists, including systems installers, were $40,430 in 2004, according to 2006 data from the U.S. Bureau of Labor Statistics.

Employment: Job prospects are excellent as our society's computer infrastructure is expected to grow rapidly.

Education: An associate's degree with an emphasis on courses covering computer systems installation can provide the training necessary to gain entry-level employment in this field.

Work Environment: To check and set up connections, you may work at desks as well as under them in clean, well-lit offices.

The computer is an integral part of our lives—at home, work, and school. But not everyone has the technical know-how to install and set up systems. That's where the computer systems installer steps in. Systems installers are the technicians who are responsible for designing, installing, and supporting an organization's local-area network (LAN), wide-area network (WAN), Internet, and intranet systems. Installers also come to the aid of individuals who are connecting their home computer systems. Once a system is installed, these professionals may also offer support services, maintaining the hardware and software. They may monitor a network to ensure its availability to system users and analyze any problems that come up.

In many ways, systems installers are on the frontlines in keeping our computerized world up and running. While many techies sit behind a computer designing software, programming, and creating Web sites, these experts are on the go. They set up computers in cubicles, crawl under desks, connect equipment, run wiring through ceilings, maintain servers, and test networks. They may travel to different client locations or pay house calls to private individuals. These technicians typically work closely with fellow employees to answer questions and give advice. They listen carefully to user problems and make fast decisions to get systems up and running the right way.

For many firms, networks and connectivity are their lifeblood. Installers make sure computers are equipped with all the necessary software and plugged into in-house channels as well as the Internet. At the end of the day, workers may back up data to a main server. Again, the systems installer shoulders the responsibility, making sure employees can do just that. Vigilance is a priority. These technicians keep a close watch on the performance of existing networks and regularly survey users to determine future system updates. On a daily basis, they make systems adjustments to assure optimal performance. The career combines computer savvy, problem-solving, and manual labor. Occasionally, these specialists have to log long hours and perform under pressure as time is of the essence. Malfunctioning computers can cost businesses big bucks. So installers move fast to solve glitches and set up required equipment. Systems installers are familiar with all departments at a major firm. Their handiwork is in demand wherever there are computers—in manufacturing, editorial offices, customer service, accounting, purchasing, and beyond.

Although installers work in a many different industries, a significant percentage are employed in scientific and technical-services industries. Others work for companies that handle administrative and support services: banks, government agencies, insurance companies, educational institutions, and wholesale and retail vendors of computers, office equipment, appliances, and home electronic equipment. Employers range from small startup companies to industry leaders.

On the Job

As a systems installer, you will usually work around 40 hours a week but sometimes put in overtime to take care of sudden setbacks or get computers up and running to meet business demands. You may be required to take on a night shift or be on call for emergencies. You're usually not in your office but traveling to trouble spots that require your expertise.

Since you'll often be working at someone else's desk, conditions can be less than ideal. The job demands physical exertion as well. You're often getting your hands dirty—lifting, carrying, stretching, and reaching into inaccessible places. As a result, you can dress more casually than your colleagues, but you will still be expected to maintain a standard of neatness and professionalism.

Systems installers have considerable opportunities for self-employment handling repairs and upgrades for home consumers and small businesses. Part of the job is keeping up-to-date with ever-changing software and operating systems.

Typical daily tasks include

- following diagrams and written instructions to set up systems or repair defects in them
- configuring computer systems
- running network applications to support systems and users
- reconfiguring systems to support new applications
- setting up new users
- troubleshooting system and network problems and diagnosing and fixing hardware/software problems

- finding solutions to problems, whether by creating a desktop shortcut or fixing a major defect in an operating system
- providing support documentation, including procedural documentation
- replacing parts as required
- testing and evaluating new technology
- conducting electrical safety checks on computer equipment

> ## "Man is the lowest-cost, 150-pound, nonlinear, all-purpose computer system which can be mass-produced by unskilled labor."
> ### —NASA

Keys to Success

To be a successful systems installer, you need

- an understanding of operating systems, networks, servers, database structures, and the World Wide Web
- a customer-service orientation
- excellent logic and troubleshooting skills
- strong technical aptitude
- the ability to work independently or as part of a team
- excellent written and oral communication skills
- physical strength, mobility, and manual dexterity
- excellent listening and questioning skills combined with the ability to interact confidently with clients to establish what the problem is and explain the solution
- patience and persistence
- a detail orientation
- excellence at meeting deadlines

Do You Have What It Takes?

If you're interested in becoming a systems installer you not only need strong problem-solving and analytical aptitudes, you'll also need excellent communication skills because troubleshooting and helping others are vital parts of the job. The constant interaction with other computer personnel, customers, and employees will require you to be able communicate effectively on paper, via e-mail, or in person. Strong writing skills may also useful if you're asked to prepare manuals for employees or clients. Some employers look for job candidates who set up their own computer systems, install their own software, and are creative thinkers. They often seek job candidates with a genuine curiosity about how things work, who like to solve puzzles, and who are thorough about following the proper procedures.

A Typical Day at Work

As an entry-level technician, you may take care of routine maintenance and monitoring of computer systems, typically working behind the scenes in an organization. A typical day begins by checking and prioritizing work requests and responding to emergencies. You spend part of your morning writing up some technical documentation, such as instructions for attaching a network printer. However, you should be prepared for interruptions from users who need immediate support. Once you've resolved and documented each problem, you get back to your printer document. Later, you catch up with a colleague to discuss plans for the expansion of the computer system. At lunch, you receive a call from a coworker who is having problems setting up a new high-speed color printer. You try to resolve this issue over the phone by talking him through some possible solutions. You agree to stop by his office to check on how he did. This kind of interruption is commonplace. During the afternoon you start to work on a scheduled hardware upgrade. This needs to be done when colleagues are away from their desks at meetings so the computers are free. That afternoon, you finish the work requests from the morning that were not necessarily urgent but need to be finished by the end of the day. Before the end of the day, you find a quiet time to answer all the e-mails in your inbox. Finally, before leaving the office you make sure you have all the disks together for a software upgrade installation that's scheduled for the next morning.

How to Break In

Companies are looking for technicians who are knowledgeable about the function and administration of networks. These computer networks are increasingly a crucial element of any business, so skilled systems installers are highly valued. Those looking for an entry-level position will probably find more opportunities with large corporations and other major organizations that have a significant demand for computer services. The completion of a certification-training program, offered by a variety of vendors and product makers, will help you qualify. It's also helpful to gain hands-on experience in the field as an intern or volunteer.

Two-Year Training

A career in this field requires both classroom instruction and field experience. Courses of study will include the principles of technical support, desktop operating systems, fiber optic cable systems, wireless networking, IP (internet protocol) telephony, network security, environmental issues, and more. The prospective student should also look for a program that includes an internship with experienced computer installers and repair technicians. A graduate should leave an associate's-degree program with the ability to perform installations, configurations, diagnostics, preventive maintenance, and basic networking. Many two-year schools prepare students for certification as a technician.

What to Look For in a School

When considering a two-year school, be sure to ask these questions:

☞ Is the computer equipment up-to-date?

☞ Are the faculty certified? Are their certifications current?

☞ If you're interested in the circuitry of computers, does the college offer electrical and computer engineering courses?

☞ Will you have the chance to specialize, in artificial intelligence or databases, for example?

☞ What employment opportunities are available to graduates?

The Future

Jobs for systems installers are expected to increase faster than the average for all occupations through 2014, according to 2006 data from the U.S. Bureau of Labor Statistics, as organizations continue to adopt increasingly sophisticated technology and integrate it into their systems. Employment will be generated by the ongoing expansion of the computer system design and related services. Prospects are best for postsecondary graduates who are up-to-date on the latest skills and technologies.

Did You Know?

Worms are devious programs that spread through e-mail and the Internet and can destroy data and disrupt computer systems. Systems installers often equip computers with protection against worms.

Interview with a Professional:
Q&A

Scott Gamble

Lead systems administrator, Cdigix Inc.,
Seattle, Washington

Q: *How did you get started?*

A: My dad was a computer nut, so I grew up with it. Our first actual PC was an IBM Clone—a Franklin Ace 1000. When I was 25, I wanted to work on computers, but I needed money to buy one so I could learn what to work on. I posted on Craigslist for people who wanted to donate old computers so I could have them to work with and learn on. I picked up a lot of junk computers. Only one out of five was usable. However, on that rebuilt machine, I was able to install a copy of Linux and started learning Linux from the ground up. Then I posted on Craigslist again, this time for tech repair jobs—anything I could get my paws on. This went on for about a year with minimal success. I then signed up for the network design and administration program at Seattle Central Community College. There I learned about industry certifications. I took my CompTIA Net+ and CompTIA Linux+ certification exams within three months of each other. In the program at SCCC, we were also strongly encouraged to get internships to further our education with real-world experience. This is what I feel was the best thing I ever did: I posted online for an apprenticeship—not an internship. I was looking for a mentor—someone who's been in the industry and didn't mind showing me the ropes.

Jeff Thoren had a small consultancy and needed someone with more Linux experience than he had to round out his skill set. I wasn't great, but I was more knowledgeable than anyone else in his shop. It wasn't much, just a toehold, but I tried to make the best of it. I apprenticed directly under him for almost two years. I will forever be grateful for his tutelage.

Q: *What techniques helped most in your job search?*

A: Technologically I focused on one or two areas and really tried to become as expert in them as I could. First and foremost I'm a "Linux Guy"—I prefer it. If you want to get more specific than that, I like e-mail servers and firewalls. I'm also a decent networking/Cisco guy. I am not a CCNA (Cisco Certified Network Associate) yet, but I will be within the next six months. In learning how to implement Linux solutions, I've also had to learn how to smoothly integrate them into Windows networks.

(continued on next page)

(continued from previous page)

This gave me a great deal of experience with Windows, Exchange, IIS, and Active Directory.

I am also a great "white-boarder" and a good public speaker. White-boarder isn't a real word, but I'm making it one. Give me a whiteboard and a fistful of dry-erase markers, and I can draw and diagram some extremely complicated systems for some very non-techie people in a way they can understand. My ability to whiteboard confidently helps me greatly, even in interviews.

Q: *What's a typical day like?*

A: I don't really have a typical day. Some days are project-based, while others are spent responding to e-mails and putting out small user fires. Some days are spent consulting or briefing executives on the technical details of a project, or working with the developers to help put a product into place. Some days I spend ordering new equipment or learning some new technology (software or hardware), or organizing my CDs, or hiring/training an intern. The variety is endless.

Q: *What's your advice for those starting a career?*

A: Pick one or two areas and become an expert in them, but still gain as much breadth of experience and exposure as you can. This sounds contradictory but it's really not. The times I've had the most success is when I knew one or two things better than most and was given opportunities to demonstrate some mastery in those areas. As time went on, more opportunities were offered.

You also need to be competitive—if only with yourself. If you don't know a thing then, challenge yourself to find it out. Learn it. Then challenge yourself to learn it better than most others will.

Practice your whiteboarding. The ability to depict even simple mechanisms visually will be of tremendous value. Your superiors are hiring you because you know what you're doing and will look to you to explain to them what's involved, so they can make good decisions as leaders.

Seek out an apprenticeship. You just have to find someone who's willing to help you figure it out and provide the opportunities.

Lastly—and this is probably the most important—don't make promises you can't keep. If you say you'll be there at 10:00, be there at 10:00. If you say you will be done in an hour, be done in an hour. If that means you have to get there by 9:45, do it. Build in extra time because everything takes longer than you think it's going to. This is a universal fact of life in this industry.

Q: *What's the best part of working in systems installation?*

A: I like being the one who makes good on the faith they put in me to do a quality job. I like being the go-to guy.

Job Seeking Tips

See the suggestions below and turn to Appendix A for advice on résumés and interviewing.

✔ Familiarize yourself with different computer systems.

✔ Earn certification. Check with the Computing Technology Industry Association (http://www.comptia.org).

✔ Get experience through an internship or volunteer work.

✔ Research industries where there are the most job opportunities.

Career Connections

For more on careers in systems installations, contact the following organizations.

Association of Computer Support Specialists http://www.acss.org

Association of Support Professionals http://www.asponline.com

System Administrators Guild http://www.sage.org

National Workforce Center for Emerging Technologies http://www.nwcet.org

Computing Technology Industry Association http://www.comptia.org

Associate's Degree Programs

Here are a few two-year schools offering quality programs related to systems installation:

Seattle Central Community College, Seattle, Washington

Capitol Community College, Hartford, Connecticut

Delmar Community College, Corpus Christi, Texas

Alexandra Community College, Alexandria, Minnesota

Financial Aid

Here is one scholarship related to systems installation. Many two-year schools offer awards for study in this area. For more on financial aid for two-year students, turn to Appendix B.

Computer, Science, Engineering, and Mathematics Scholarships— CSEMS. This is a program funded by the National Science Foundation. If you qualify, you may receive up to $3,125 per year to help defray the cost of education and your living expenses.   http://www.nsf.gov/her/rec/csemslinks.jsp

Related Careers

Computer programmers, computer software engineers, computer systems analysts, computer scientists, and database administrators.

Computer Repair Technician

Vital Statistics

Salary: Computer support technicians, such as repair specialists, earn an average annual salary of $43,380, according to 2006 figures from the U.S. Bureau of Labor Statistics.

Employment: Government economists expect job growth for computer support specialists to be faster than the average for all professions through 2014.

Education: Courses in computer science, business, and communications are all required to become a repair technician.

Work Environment: Since repair technicians fix other people's machines, they move from place to place and work in a lot of different environments.

Do friends and family members call you when they can't figure out what's wrong with their computers? Do you get a sense of satisfaction when you've solved their problems? Do you like to keep up with the latest hardware and software products? If so, you'd probably be a terrific "go-to" tech at a small company or perfect heading the repair desk of a large corporation.

In the last 10 years, computers have become fundamental to all business transactions. Computer networks have spread through homes and businesses at hyper-speeds. People invest big bucks in these systems, so when something goes wrong, they want to get them fixed—and fast. It's no wonder the repair expert is in such high demand and earning high salaries. The highest-paid technicians can earn $70,000, according to 2006 data from the Bureau of Labor Statistics.

Whether it's a hard drive that crashes or just a mouse that stops working, technicians have to have the training to tackle problems great and small. A lot of the work—rewiring, installing memory, connecting cables—requires manual dexterity. But a computer repair technician also acts as a guru of sorts, dispensing how-to wisdom over the phone and via e-mails. When panicked workers call, distressed from dealing with malfunctioning equipment, technicians know how to communicate and talk them down. They calmly relay instructions and assure coworkers that they will pull through.

Technicians know computers inside and out. They understand mainframes, servers, and personal computers, as well as printers and disk drives. They can diagnose shortcomings with monitors, keyboards, and mice. They need to be familiar with the networks and applications that are installed on the hardware as well, since they may be called on to check or repair the software. While technicians run automated diagnostics programs to pin-point ailments, computers often cannot heal themselves. The repair techs roll up their sleeves and perform hands-on adjustments and maintenance. As masters of their computer universe, they may be asked to write training manuals or teach coworkers how to use new hardware and software.

Repair technicians work directly for companies or for hardware and software vendors. They may also command the help-desk or support services at a firm, dispensing computer advice to clients. Many techs are self-employed and take on assignments on a project-to-project basis.

On the Job

Of all the tech careers, this one may be the most physical. When equipment breaks down, you travel to a client's workplace or other location to make the necessary repairs. You may even be an assigned territory and perform preventive maintenance on a regular basis for the clients in that area. When at a work site, you apply your trade in well-lighted, comfortable offices, but you may have to crawl under desks to check wiring or climb ladders to run cables through a drop ceiling. Sometimes you can't make the fix on-site, so you have to lug a hard drive back to your headquarters.

While some techs put in a regular 40-hour week, many push well beyond normal hours as emergencies never sleep. As a repair tech, you receive distress calls via pager or cell phone at all hours. You may put in evening or weekend time to get vital systems back up and running again.

Long stretches can go by where it's just the computer and you, applying your analytical skills to solve the problem at hand. Solutions can require cracking into the wiring of a monitor or hard drive to replace parts. When not wrestling with the computers themselves, you're dealing with customers or coworkers—face-to-face, on the phone, or via e-mail. Communication is essential. In some ways, you're like a doctor who must carefully listen to a patient's problems and then be ready to dispense helpful advice. You may employ some psychology as well to calm the frayed nerves of those who have suffered a technological mishap.

 ## Keys to Success

To be a successful computer repair technician, you need
- excellent communication skills
- superior problem-solving abilities
- flexibility and adaptability
- interest in and willingness to learn about working with systems and with people
- ability to gather data and information
- good eyesight

❦ manual dexterity
❦ general electronics and computer knowledge

Do You Have What It Takes?

If you're a do-it-yourself, fix-it type of person, this may be a good career choice for you. This occupation requires that you have a natural interest in how things work. Education-wise, the novice repair tech must learn the basics of electronics. If you decide to specialize—in mainframes, for example—you'll need extra training. Increasingly, employers prefer workers who are certified as repair technicians for the equipment they support. To get certified, you'll need to pass a qualifying exam corresponding to your level of training and experience. Many two-year colleges, as well as industry organizations and companies, offer certification.

One of the most important things to remember in this career is how quickly the industry changes. The successful repair tech never stops learning and stays abreast of all the latest technology by reading current journals, visiting pertinent Web sites, and attending meetings of professional associations.

In addition to technical smarts, you must have people skills. If you're good at listening to others and giving advice that applies directly to their problems, you will have a step up in this career. Techs provide clear explanations and directions in writing as well as in person and on the phone. A certain amount of physical stamina is part of this job, and to work with the components used in computer design, good eyesight and color perception are important.

> ## "The problem with troubleshooting is that trouble shoots back."
> ### —Author unknown

How to Break In

When hiring repair technicians, most companies look for curiosity, initiative, technical knowledge and skills, and personality. Be sure to go on interviews armed with a lot of good questions. If possible, be prepared to tell a story about some problem you've solved, whether it's computer-related or not.

Hands-on experience can be very valuable. Take advantage of internships that your school offers. If you can't get an internship, try to find a local organization that will take you on as a volunteer. Internships and volunteer work can gain you some impressive references.

Finally, check out what certifications are currently in demand and take one. If your school doesn't offer them, you can get lots of information about other sources on the Web.

A Typical Day at Work

As an entry-level repair technician, you may just deal with personal computers or peripheral equipment to start. With a little experience, however, you may be called on to maintain more sophisticated systems, such as networking equipment and servers.

To a large extent, breakdowns and other service requirements that pop up determine your daily routine. They may be reported to you directly or through a supervisor who receives and routes tickets according to the expertise and availability of the techs on staff. Most repair technicians carry over some low-priority problems from one day to the next.

A lot of your day will be spent interacting with users at their sites. You may be taking a few elevator rides, traveling from floor to floor and from desk to desk, or you may be in the car for parts of your day, driving to various company locations. You might not be able to solve all problems on your own, so you may call your company's help desk from time to time. They may be able to provide support from other techs for those unusual or difficult issues, or they may arrange to bring you a spare part that's needed in a hurry.

No job is without its mundane tasks—a tech must complete clerical work, log in hours for each job, and write up service reports, time sheets, and expense reports. At most companies, you are supplied with a laptop you can use to complete all these documents while you're still at the user's location.

Two-Year Training

Two-year programs for technicians may go under the banner of "computer engineering technology." They usually provide students with in-depth experience in computer installation, configuration, troubleshooting, computer repair, operating systems, and basic networking. Associate-degree programs prepare students to take exams that will certify them as repairers/installers. Certification may be in A+, Network+, or Microsoft.

Along with basic repair classes, two-year students take courses covering database management, Web development, applications of information systems, network security, and desktop support. Outside the technical realm, students should hone their business and communication skills. Related majors include computer programming, computer or electrical engineering, computer systems analysis, or electronics technology.

What to Look For in a School

When considering a two-year school, be sure to ask these questions:

☞ Does the computer science or the electrical engineering department offer the program? How does that affect the program's focus?

☞ Are labs equipped with state-of-the-art electronics?

☞ What internships and other hands-on learning opportunities will you have?

☞ Are the faculty members certified? Are their certifications up-to-date?

☞ Do courses prepare you for certification exams?

☞ How is the job placement office and employment rate of recent grads?

The Future

Technology requires regular upgrades, maintenance, and repairs, and businesses and nonprofits depend on technicians to get these jobs done. Opportunities for support specialists are expected to boom, especially considering reports showing that there are not enough technicians to meet the demand. Job prospects should be best for college graduates who are up-to-date with the latest skills and technologies, and have supplemented their classroom studies with relevant work experience.

Did You Know?

Computers are more reliable. According to a survey by the Gartner market research group, failure rates for desktop computers and portable notebooks have improved over time.

Job Seeking Tips

See the suggestions below and turn to Appendix A for advice on résumés and interviewing.

✔ Get references through an internship or volunteer job.

✔ Be open to working as a freelancer—these jobs often lead to full-time positions.

✔ Keep in touch with other computer professionals—they often know of job leads.

✔ Join professional organizations.

✔ Scour Web site employment pages that cater to IT experts.

Interview with a Professional:
Q&A

Keith Bailey

Instructor, Cecil County School of Technology, and
computer repair technician, Elkton, Maryland

Q: *How did you get started?*

A: I was required to do a work/study class for my degree and signed on
with one of my instructors [Ed Boas] who had his own computer business.
He was impressed by my work in class and asked me to help him on a couple of large projects he was working on. After finishing my work/study
class, he asked me to stay with him. I ended up working for him for 10
years full time, and I still do some part-time work for him.

Q: *What's a typical day like?*

A: In the computer repair business I don't think there is a typical day, but
we started at 9:00 a.m. each morning. We would continue work left from
the day before or gather the items needed to go out for service calls on site
and deliver items ordered by customers. We would eat lunch when we had
time; many times this was not until late afternoon, if we were busy. Sometimes I might need to stop what I was doing and wait on a customer who
wanted advice on buying something computer-related—anything from a
game or business application to a new computer system. Weather would
also play a big factor in how business went. On a snowy day or rainy day
the phone would ring off the hook with people calling for tech support.
Everyone was using their computers since they could not go outside. A bad
thunderstorm was also always good for business because customers' computers would get damaged in the storm [from power surges, etc.]. On the
other side of that, people don't use their computers as much when the
weather is nice and sunny. That's when there is panic for us—when there is
no business.

Q: *What's your advice for those starting a career?*

A: For those trying to break in, it's important to understand that you are
not going to make the big money at first. You need to put some time in and
get experience. Having a second computer at home to try out and practice
things on is helpful. There is a lot of pressure to perform—you need to get
it right the first time. Also, don't sell yourself short if you are doing work for
people you know. Have a set hourly rate and stick to it.

(continued on next page)

(continued from previous page)

Q: *What's the best part of being a computer repair technician?*

A: I like the challenge of finding the problem and then fixing it. I also enjoy working with my hands and helping the customers. There is always something new, and it is not the same thing every day.

Career Connections

For more on careers in computer repair, contact the following organizations.

Association of Computer Support Specialists http://www.acss.org

Association of Support Professionals http://www.asponline.com

National Workforce Center for Emerging Technologies http://www.nwcet.org

Associate's Degree Programs

Here are a few two-year schools offering quality computer repair programs:

Tompkins Cortland Community College, Dryden, New York

Cecil Community College, North East, Maryland

Scottsdale Community College, Scottsdale, Arizona

Glendale Community College, Glendale, California

Florida Community College, Jacksonville, Florida

Financial Aid

Here are a few scholarships related to computer repair. Many two-year schools offer their own financial awards for students pursuing an associate's degree in computer repair. For more on financial aid for two-year students, turn to Appendix B.

EasyAid's Computer Science Scholarship This $500 scholarship is for students who are majoring in any type of degree that involves computers and computer science. You are eligible if you will be attending any type of postsecondary educational institution in the 2006–2007 or 2007–2008 school year.   http://www.easyaid.com

NSF Scholarships in Science, Technology, Engineering, and Mathematics This program makes grants to institutions of higher education to support scholarships for academically talented, financially needy students, enabling them to enter the workforce following completion of an associate's, baccalaureate, or graduate-evel degree in science and

engineering disciplines. Grantee institutions are responsible for selecting scholarship recipients.   http://www.nsf.gov

Google Anita Borg Memorial Scholarship This $10,000 scholarship is
for outstanding female undergraduate and graduate students complet-
ing their degrees in computer science and related fields.
http://www.google.com/anitaborg/

Related Careers

Computer hardware engineers, computer programmers, computer software
engineers, computer systems analysts, and database administrators.

Wireless Technician

Vital Statistics

Salary: The average annual earnings for senior electronics technicians, including those who handle wireless systems, range from $46,000 to $60,000, according to the U.S. Bureau of Labor Statistics.

Employment: Wireless technicians are in huge demand. According to Robert Half Technology, one of the most in demand technical skills within IT departments is wireless network management.

Education: Courses in networking and routing technology are especially important; in addition to a degree, many jobs require certification in wireless technologies.

Work Environment: Wireless technicians generally work at computer terminals in offices or retail stores.

In many ways, one of the hottest areas in technology is invisible. Wireless communications allow us to transmit voice messages, data, and other signals through the air without physically connecting senders to receivers with cables or wires. And the technology is spreading at lightning speed. Cellular telephones, personal digital assistants, and wireless networking are all prime examples of our new wireless world.

Sending signals through the airwaves is nothing new. Radios were really the first wireless gadgets, and early radio was even referred to as "the wireless." TV, garage door openers, and remote controls all operate off wireless transmissions. But in today's computer and IT world, the wireless technician often deals with WLANs, or wireless local-area networks. A WLAN links two or more computers without using wires, and many firms are linking their computers in this way. You will find these networks at large college campuses, retail firms, health care corporations, warehouses, and more.

Those with home computers primarily use wireless to connect to the Web. They need to install a "hub" that connects to high-speed Internet. Then, the hub puts out a signal that can be detected by, for instance, a laptop equipped with a receiver—called an "airport" on some computers. With wireless laptops, people can sit poolside, in the kitchen, and on their beds and tap into the World Wide Web. Hotels, cafes, and other businesses have been offering wireless service, sometimes for a small fee. Many cities and municipalities are getting into the wireless game as well, providing Wi-Fi (wireless fidelity) connections outdoors and free for public use.

Many users carry several wireless devices at all times, each typically with different operating systems, display types, markup (coding) languages, scripting capabilities, and wireless networks—such as CDPD (Cellular Digital Packet Data), Mobitex, Motient, and SMS (Short Message Service). One technology, called third generation (3G) wireless access, lets users download music, videos, and other content directly into their cell phones. Businesses, schools, and government offices are all face the challenge of hiring enough trained professionals to support wireless devices and services.

As a wireless communications technician you may be installing, testing, adjusting, maintaining, and repairing defective equipment and components in order to ensure that the correct calibration and frequencies are met. This can translate into everything from attaching antennae or satellite dishes to the sides of customers' buildings to tracking customer data with the help of client tracking systems or instructing customers on the proper use of cellular phones and other equipment. Securing wireless networks is a major concern because information transmitted through the airwaves could be intercepted and used for illegal purposes.

Some wireless technicians handle sales or customer service, helping clients understand the new and varied types of services offered by telecommunications providers. Other techs focus on developing and marketing the software or middleware needed to power the new wireless devices. This wireless niche requires the mastery of computer markup languages—XML (Extensible Markup Language), WML (Wireless Markup Language), HTML (Hypertext Markup Language), HDML (Handheld Device Markup Language) or VoiceML. Professionals in this field may specialize in sophisticated data compression and encryption/protocol translation; functions that allow Web, WAP (wireless application protocol), and voice interactions to all blend into one session.

In this fast-paced industry, new systems are continually being designed, built, and maintained. From the big telecommunications firms that are developing wireless products to the businesses seeking expertise in setting up their own wireless office networks, employers are desperately seeking qualified workers, making wireless one of the hottest career fields in the computer and information technology universe.

On the Job

As a wireless technician, you can be sure of steady, year-round work. If you service equipment, you may be required to put in overtime occasionally and report in at a moment's notice, especially during emergencies like floods and hurricanes.

The wireless tech applies the trade mostly indoors, often in a telecommunication company's central office or a retail store. Sometimes, specialized receivers and transmitters have to be connected outside as well. The job requires some local travel to maintain the equipment that transmits signals. Those who field questions at a help desk work at a video display terminal in pleasant, well-lighted, air-conditioned surroundings.

Those in development focus on research and improving systems. They may study the latest cell phones and wireless networks and figure out ways to increase their speed and reliability. They prepare specifications, build new prototypes, and write instruction manuals. Wireless techs in the field consult with clients and try to meet their needs. These professionals may install networks or resolve problems with current systems and products. All wireless positions require specific technical training to apply science, information, and engineering principles. All techs have the ability to schedule, budget, plan, work with others, and communicate effectively.

Keys to Success

To be a successful wireless technician, you need
- a strong computer background
- a passion for mathematics and science
- analytical ability
- problem-solving skills
- independence
- a customer service orientation
- excellent oral and written communication skills
- attention to detail
- superior eyesight and color vision
- manual dexterity
- a fast, methodical approach to work

Do You Have What It Takes?

Are you always curious about the latest innovations in electronic devices and gadgets? Wireless could be for you. For starters, you'll need a strong background in math, science, and technology. High school courses in algebra, geometry, physics, English, and trigonometry are especially helpful. Eventually, you'll have to get a higher education to master basic wireless technology. Entry-level employees have familiarity with different computer software and strong communication skills. This field is changing fast, so you really have to be someone who is a "lifetime learner," ready to study new technologies as they emerge.

On the job, you must be accurate, thorough, responsible, and safety-conscious. You should also enjoy solving problems and working at a fast pace. Since you'll be interacting with customers and coworkers, it pays to be a people person. But when you're at a client site, you'll be mainly working on your own, so you'll need to be able to manage your time and make decisions independently.

A Typical Day at Work

Wireless techs are troubleshooters. If you embark on this career, you may start your day by checking a security report and scanning the entire WLAN system to make sure everything's in working order. You reboot any equipment that's not working and make sure the network is up and functioning properly. You want to check that all employees are able to log into the wireless network. Part of your day can be devoted to setting up and installing equipment and making sure all connectivity issues are resolved. If your firm operates offices outside of your headquarters, you may take a few short car trips to support those colleagues.

If you happen to be working for a telecommunications company, you may consult with a "testing team." These coworkers look for dropped calls and dead spots that have been reported by customers and then report problems to you.

When working with testing teams, you may be carrying several phones in your vehicle that have had their software adjusted to allow detailed logging and control features. You also carry equipment to test data connections and at least two laptops, one for voice calls and one for data connections. They should both be connected to a GPS system so that the car's exact position is recorded along with all the other data.

Calls are made from all of the phones back to a set of computers at the office. A set recording is used to test the overall voice quality. Because the software knows the quality of the original clip, it's a simple process to tell the quality of the call. The computer also makes calls to the wireless phone in the car, so that you'll hear it ring regularly.

Wireless technician jobs can be very diverse but all draw on fast thinking, analytical skills, computer-savvy, communications, and people skills. When your technological skills are good and sharp, they have a way of supporting your people skills.

How to Break In

Credentials required differ by region, level of position, and employer. Companies look for workers with various combinations of skills in computer programming and software design, as well as voice telephone technology, laser and fiber optic technology, wireless technology, and data compression.

Applicants with some real-world experience have an edge. One way to get this hands-on training is through an internship at your school. Another way is to get certified. "Performance-based certifications can give you an edge in the absence of much on-the-job experience," says Peter Childers, Vice President of Global Learning Services at Red Hat. Cisco Systems, for example, offers its own WLAN certification exam. If you lack experience you can also try doing some volunteer work. Churches and schools are excellent places to start looking for opportunities to gain experience.

Activities outside the IT field are also valued. "In today's climate, companies are looking for people that have other skills, like customer service and project management," says Childers. "Even something like working in a call center and getting an award for customer service can help your ability to present yourself positively."

Two-Year Training

To get into this field you'll need to major in computer systems networking and telecommunications. Your courses will cover the design, installation, and improvement of computer networks and related software. In your networking classes, you'll focus on the basic use of hardware and software and the special needs of local area networks (LANs). One topic in this area of study is routing technology, which moves information between computers. By the time you graduate, you'll know how to expand the capabilities of networks already in place and how to build new ones. Typical two-year programs cover concepts such as radio frequency, two-way land mobile, microwave, cellular, telephone, fiber optics, satellite, radar, commercial broadcast, and data networking applications.

What to Look For in a School

When considering a two-year school, be sure to ask these questions:

☞ Does the program focus more on preparing students for further education or for the workforce?

☞ Will the classes help you prepare for certification exams?

☞ Are instructors certified and actively working in the field?

☞ Does the program have state-of-the-art classrooms and computer labs?

☞ Are hands-on learning activities a regular part of your studies?

☞ Does the program coordinate with local companies and organizations to provide internships?

☞ What are recent graduates doing now?

The Future

According to 2006 information from the U.S. Bureau of Labor Statistics, networking technology is expected to be one of the fastest-growing areas of employment through 2014, but you'll need to get certified to compete for the best jobs in the field. The demands for wireless are growing exponentially as consumers demand more of the freedom and flexibility that wireless can provide.

Interview with a Professional:
Q&A

Danielle J. Liebhard

Motor-generator set sales, Kato Engineering Inc.,
Mankato, Minnesota

Q: *How did you get started?*

A: My first job out of high school was working for a company called Solitra, Inc. Solitra was a Finnish-based wireless technology company that specialized in RF [radio frequency] filters, subsystems, and components. I got the job as the result of excelling on an aptitude test. Since the company needed technicians and what they were training their technicians to do was very hands on, they gave me a chance.

I eventually decided to go back to school. I graduated with a degree in wireless communications, as an electronic technician with a amateur radio license, marine radio operator permit. I am also a certified electronic technician through the ETA [Electronic Technician Association].

After graduation I started working for a company that manufactured flex circuits. While working there, I was trained in CADD [computer-aided design and drafting] operation. I would read customer supplied drawings of the specific flex circuit desired, work the basic design into CADD, and—while working closely with sales and engineering—developed a method of estimating the number of individual flex circuits that could be manufactured on a single copper sheet. This is when I really got the sales bug and realized this was something I wanted to incorporate into my career.

Q: *What's a typical day like?*

A: My days are anything but typical. Each day is different from the last. I of course do quotations for my customers, enter purchase orders, track my M-G [motor-generator] set orders in production, attend production meetings, but I also attend shows and conventions that advertise our product line for future orders. This November I will be working the booth at the 2006 International Work Boat Show. Our M-G sets are also used for naval purposes. Back in September I visited a customer out in Seattle for a large order that was recently received. So there is also travel involved in what I do. You have to stay on top of things because I am the point of contact for the customer. I am the customer's voice to production and engineering.

Q: *What's your advice for those starting a career?*

A: I would have to say using all resources available and sticking with what works. I used the Minnesota Work Force Center extensively. They offer a lot more than job listings. The Work Force Center can help you with your résumé, one-on-one career counseling, etc. Also, don't be afraid to ask questions and to ask for help; there is more out there than you probably think there is.

Give it a chance. You never know what might happen in whatever you decide to pursue. What you decide to do in life can turn into something better then you ever imagined it to be. But be ambitious, involved, and interested.

Q: *What's the best part of working in this field?*

A: The best part about working in wireless technology is the fact that you are not limited in wireless technology. Electronics is electronics wherever you go. I don't work for a wireless company, but I am very capable of doing what I do.

> "The wireless telegraph is not difficult to understand. The ordinary telegraph is like a very long cat. You pull the tail in New York, and it meows in Los Angeles. The wireless is the same, only without the cat."
> —Albert Einstein, physicist

Did You Know?

A vicar in Cardiff, Wales, is offering wireless broadband access from the pews of his church, alongside traditional weddings, christenings, and Sunday services.

Job Seeking Tips

Follow these suggestions and turn to Appendix A for tips on résumés and interviewing.

✔ Get certified.
✔ Keep up-to-date.
✔ Research companies in the field.
✔ To see who's hiring, check online or attend career fairs.
✔ Keep in touch with faculty, classmates, and those you meet in the course of your job search.

Career Connections

For more on careers in wireless technology, contact the following organizations.

Society of Cable Telecommunications Engineers http://www.scte.org

International Society of Certified Electronics Technicians http://www.iscet.org

Global Wireless Education Consortium http://www.gwec.org

ACES (Association of Communications and Electronics Schools) International http://www.acesinternational.org

CTIA—The Wireless Association http://www.ctia.org

Silicon Valley-China Wireless Technology Association http://www.svcwireless.org/sponsorships/index.html

US Telecom http://www.ustelecom.org

Associate's Degree Programs

Here are a few two-year schools offering quality wireless telecommunications programs:

South Central College, Fairbault, Minnesota

Skyline Community College, San Bruno, California

Bellevue Community College, Bellevue, Washington

Brookdale Community College, Lincroft, New Jersey

Rend Lake College, Ina, Illinois

Financial Aid

Here are a few scholarship sources to get you started. Turn to Appendix B for information about financial aid for two-year students.

Society of Cable Telecommunications Engineers This group provides scholarships to assist members and their children in their continued pursuit of knowledge.   http://www.scte.org

Telecommunications Association of Michigan Foundation, Inc. Scholarship Fund This organization promotes educational and scientific advancement by helping individuals obtain instruction or training to improve and develop their capabilities. http://www.telecommich.org/scholarshis

The Foundation for Rural Education and Development The foundation awards the Internships in Telecommunications Scholarship worth $1,000 to rural America's best and brightest students. http://www.fred.org

The Golden West Scholarship Program This South Dakota telecommunications firm awards $1,000 scholarships to graduating seniors at 45 area high schools. http://www.goldenwest.com/corporate/scholarships/guidelines.php

Related Careers

Computer hardware engineers, computer software engineers, computer support specialists, database administrators, engineering technicians, and network administrators.

Appendix A
Tools for Career Success

When 20-year-old Justin Schulman started job-hunting for a position as a fitness trainer—his first step toward managing a fitness facility—he didn't mess around. "I immediately opened the Yellow Pages and started calling every number listed under health and fitness, inquiring about available positions," he recalls. Schulman's energy and enterprise paid off: He wound up with interviews that led to several offers of part-time work.

Schulman's experience highlights an essential lesson for jobseekers: There are plenty of opportunities out there, but jobs won't come to you—especially the career-oriented, well-paying ones that that you'll want to stick with over time. You've got to seek them out.

Uncover Your Interests

Whether you're in high school or bringing home a full-time paycheck, the first step toward landing your ideal job is assessing your interests. You need to figure out what makes you tick. After all, there is a far greater chance that you'll enjoy and succeed in a career that taps into your passions, inclinations, and natural abilities. That's what happened with career-changer Scott Rolfe. He was already 26 when he realized he no longer wanted to work in the food industry. "I'm an avid outdoorsman," Rolfe says, "and I have an appreciation for natural resources that many people take for granted." Rolfe turned his passions into his ideal job as a forest technician.

If you have a general idea of what your interests are, you're far ahead of the game. You may know that you're cut out for a health care career, for instance, or one in business. You can use a specific volume of Top Careers in Two Years to discover what position to target. If you are unsure of your direction, check out the whole range of volumes to see the scope of jobs available. Ask yourself, what job or jobs would I most like to do if I *already* had the training and skills? Then remind yourself that this is what your two-year training will accomplish.

You can also use interest inventories and skills-assessment programs to further pinpoint your ideal career. Your school or public librarian or guidance counselor should be able to help you locate such assessments. Web sites such as America's Career InfoNet (http://www.acinet.org) and JobWeb (http://www.jobweb.com) also offer interest inventories. Don't forget the help advisers at any two-year college can provide to target your interests. You'll find suggestions for Web sites related to specific careers at the end of each chapter in any Top Careers in Two Years volume.

Unlock Your Network

The next stop toward landing the perfect job is networking. The word may make you cringe. But networking isn't about putting on a suit, walking into a roomful of strangers, and pressing your business card on everyone. Networking is simply introducing yourself and exchanging job-related and other information that may prove helpful to one or both of you. That's what Susan Tinker-Muller did. Quite a few years ago, she struck up a conversation with a fellow passenger on her commuter train. Little did she know that the natural interest she expressed in the woman's accounts payable department would lead to news about a job opening there. Tinker-Muller's networking landed her an entry-level position in accounts payable with MTV Networks. She is now the accounts payable administrator.

Tinker-Muller's experience illustrates why networking is so important. Fully 80 percent of openings are *never* advertised, and more than half of all employees land their jobs through networking, according to the U.S. Bureau of Labor Statistics. That's 8 out of 10 jobs that you'll miss if you don't get out there and talk with people. And don't think you can bypass face-to-face conversations by posting your résumé on job sites like Monster.com and Hotjobs.com and then waiting for employers to contact you. That's so mid-1990s! Back then, tens of thousands, if not millions, of job seekers diligently posted their résumés on scores of sites. Then they sat back and waited . . . and waited . . . and waited. You get the idea. Big job sites like Monster and Hotjobs have their place, of course, but relying solely on an Internet job search is about as effective as throwing your résumé into a black hole.

Begin your networking efforts by making a list of people to talk to: teachers, classmates (and their parents), anyone you've worked with, neighbors, worship acquaintances, and anyone you've interned or volunteered with. You can also expand your networking opportunities through the student sections of industry associations (listed at the end of each chapter of Top Careers in Two Years); attending or volunteering at industry events, association conferences, career fairs; and through job-shadowing. Keep in mind that only rarely will any of the people on your list be in a position to offer you a job. But whether they know it or not, they probably know someone who knows someone who is. That's why your networking goal is not to ask for a job but the name of someone to talk with. Even when you network with an employer, it's wise to say something like, "You may not have any positions available, but might you know someone I could talk with to find out more about what it's like to work in this field?"

Also, keep in mind that networking is a two-way street. For instance, you may be talking with someone who has a job opening that isn't appropriate for you. If you can refer someone else to the employer, either person may well be disposed to help you someday in the future.

Dial-Up Help

Call your contacts directly, rather than e-mail them. (E-mails are too easy for busy people to ignore, even if they don't mean to.) Explain that you're a recent graduate in your field; that Mr. Jones referred you; and that you're wondering if you could stop by for 10 or 15 minutes at your contact's convenience to find out a little more about how the industry works. If you leave this message as a voicemail, note that you'll call back in a few days to follow up. If you reach your contact directly, expect that they'll say they're too busy at the moment to see you. Ask, "Would you mind if I check back in a couple of weeks?" Then jot down a note in your date book or set up a reminder in your computer calendar and call back when it's time. (Repeat this above scenario as needed, until you get a meeting.)

Once you have arranged to talk with someone in person, prep yourself. Scour industry publications for insightful articles; having up-to-date knowledge about industry trends shows your networking contacts that you're dedicated and focused. Then pull together questions about specific employers and suggestions that will set you apart from the job-hunting pack in your field. The more specific your questions (for instance, about one type of certification versus another), the more likely your contact will see you as an "insider," worthy of passing along to a potential employer. At the end of any networking meeting, ask for the name of someone else who might be able to help you further target your search.

Get a Lift

When you meet with a contact in person (as well as when you run into someone fleetingly), you need an "elevator speech." This is a summary of up to two minutes that introduces who you are, as well as your experience and goals. An elevator speech should be short enough to be delivered during an elevator ride with a potential employer from the ground level to a high floor. In it, it's helpful to show that 1) you know the business involved; 2) you know the company; 3) you're qualified (give your work and educational information); and 4) you're goal-oriented, dependable, and hardworking. You'll be surprised how much information you can include in two minutes. Practice this speech in front of a mirror until you have the key points down very well. It should sound natural though, and you should come across as friendly, confident, and assertive. Remember, good eye contact needs to be part of your presentation as well as your everyday approach when meeting prospective employers or leads.

Get Your Résumé Ready

In addition to your elevator speech, another essential job-hunting tool is your résumé. Basically, a résumé is a little snapshot of you in words, reduced to one 8½ x 11-inch sheet of paper (or, at most, two sheets). You need a résumé whether you're in high school, college, or the workforce, and whether you've never held a job or have had many.

At the top of your résumé should be your heading. This is your name, address, phone numbers, and your e-mail address, which can be a sticking point. E-mail addresses such as sillygirl@yahoo.com or drinkingbuddy @hotmail.com won't score you any points. In fact they're a turn-off. So if you dreamed up your address after a night on the town, maybe it's time to upgrade. (Similarly, these days potential employers often check Myspace sites, personal blogs, and Web pages. What's posted there has been known to cost candidates a job offer.)

The first section of your résumé is a concise Job Objective (e.g., "Entry-level agribusiness sales representative seeking a position with a leading dairy cooperative"). These days, with word-processing software, it's easy and smart to adapt your job objective to the position for which you're applying. An alternative way to start a résumé, which some recruiters prefer, is to re-work the Job Objective into a Professional Summary. A Professional Summary doesn't mention the position you're seeking, but instead focuses on your job strengths (e.g., "Entry-level agribusiness sales rep; strengths include background in feed, fertilizer, and related markets and ability to contribute as a member of a sales team"). Which is better? It's your call.

The body of a résumé typically starts with your Job Experience. This is a chronological list of the positions you've held (particularly the ones that will help you land the job you want). Remember: never, never any fudging. However, it is okay to include volunteer positions and internships on the chronological list, as long as they're noted for what they are.

Next comes your Education section. Note: It's acceptable to flip the order of your Education and Job Experience sections if you're still in high school or have gone straight to college and don't have significant work experience. Summarize the major courses in your degree area, any certifications you've achieved, relevant computer knowledge, special seminars, or other school-related experience that will distinguish you. Include your grade average if it's more than 3.0. Don't worry if you haven't finished your degree. Simply write that you're currently enrolled in your program (if you are).

In addition to these elements, other sections may include professional organizations you belong to and any work-related achievements, awards, or recognition you've received. Also, you can have a section for your interests, such as playing piano or soccer (and include any notable achievements regarding your interests, for instance, placed third in Midwest Regional Piano Competition). You should also note other special abilities, such as "Fluent in French" or "Designed own Web site." These sorts of activities will reflect well on you, whether or not they are job-related.

You can either include your references or simply note, "References upon Request." Be sure to ask your references permission to use their name and alert them to the fact that they may be contacted, before you include them on your résumé. For more information on résumé writing, check out Web sites such as http://www.resume.monster.com.

Craft Your Cover Letter

When you apply for a job either online or by mail, it's appropriate to include a cover letter. A cover letter lets you convey extra information about yourself that doesn't fit or isn't always appropriate in your résumé. For instance, in a cover letter, you can and should mention the name of anyone who referred you to the job. You can go into some detail about the reason you're a great match, given the job description. You also can address any questions that might be raised in the potential employer's mind (for instance, a gap in your résumé). Don't, however, ramble on. Your cover letter should stay focused on your goal: to offer a strong, positive impression of yourself and persuade the hiring manager that you're worth an interview. Your cover letter gives you a chance to stand out from the other applicants and sell yourself. In fact, 23 percent of hiring managers say a candidate's ability to relate his or her experience to the job at hand is a top hiring consideration, according to a Careerbuilder.com survey.

You can write a positive, yet concise cover letter in three paragraphs: An introduction containing the specifics of the job you're applying for; a summary of why you're a good fit for the position and what you can do for the company; and a closing with a request for an interview, contact information, and thanks. Remember to vary the structure and tone of your cover letter. For instance, don't begin every sentence with "I."

Ace Your Interview

Preparation is the key to acing any job interview. This starts with researching the company or organization you're interviewing with. Start with the firm, group, or agency's own Web site. Explore it thoroughly; read about their products and services, their history, and sales and marketing information.

Check out their news releases, links that they provide, and read up on or Google members of the management team to get an idea of what they may be looking for in their employees.

Sites such as http://www.hoovers.com enable you to research companies across many industries. Trade publications in any industry (such as *Food Industry News, Hotel Business,* and *Hospitality Technology*) are also available online or in hard copy at many college or public libraries. Don't forget to make a phone call to contacts you have in the organization to get an even better idea of the company culture.

Preparation goes beyond research, however. It includes practicing answers to common interview questions:

☞ *Tell me about yourself.* (Don't talk about your favorite bands or your personal history; give a brief summary of your background and interest in the particular job area.)

☞ *Why do you want to work here?* (Here's where your research into the company comes into play; talk about the firm's strengths and products or services.)

☞ *Why should we hire you?* (Now is your chance to sell yourself as a dependable, trustworthy, effective employee.)

☞ *Why did you leave your last job?* (This is not a talk show. Keep your answer short; never bad-mouth a previous employer. You can always say something simply such as, "It wasn't a good fit, and I was ready for other opportunities.")

Rehearse your answers but don't try to memorize them. Responses that are natural and spontaneous come across better. Trying to memorize exactly what you want to say is likely to both trip you up and make you sound robotic.

As for the actual interview, to break the ice, offer a few pleasant remarks about the day, a photo in the interviewer's office, or something else similar. Then, once the interview gets going, listen closely and answer the questions you're asked, versus making any other point that you want to convey. If you're unsure whether your answer was adequate, simply ask, "Did that answer the question?" Show respect, good energy, and enthusiasm, and be upbeat. Employers are looking for people who are enjoyable to be around, as well as good workers. Show that you have a positive attitude and can get along well with others by not bragging during the interview, overstating your experience, or giving the appearance of being too self-absorbed. Avoid one-word answers, but at the same time don't blather. If you're faced with a silence after giving your response, pause for a few seconds, and then ask, "Is there anything else you'd like me to add?" Never look at your watch or answer your cellphone during an interview.

Near the interview's end, the interviewer is likely to ask you if you have any questions. Make sure that you have a few prepared, for instance:

☞ *"Tell me about the production process."*

☞ *"What's your biggest short-term challenge?"*

☞ *"How have recent business trends affected the company?"*

☞ *"Is there anything else that I can provide you with to help you make your decision?"*

☞ *"When will you make your hiring decision?"*

During a first interview, never ask questions like, "What's the pay?" "What are the benefits?" or "How much vacation time will I get?"

Find the Right Look

Appropriate dressing and grooming is also essential to interviewing success. For business jobs and many other occupations, it's appropriate to come to an interview in a nice (not stuffy) suit. However, different fields have various dress codes. In the music business, for instance, "business casual" reigns for many jobs. This is a slightly modified look, where slacks and a jacket are just fine for a guy, and a nice skirt and blouse and jacket or sweater are acceptable for a woman. Dressing overly "cool" will usually backfire.

In general, watch all of the basics from the shoes on up (no sneakers or sandals, and no overly high heels or short skirts for women). Also avoid attention-getting necklines, girls. Keep jewelry and other "bling" to a minimum. Tattoos and body jewelry are becoming more acceptable, but if you can take out piercings (other than in your ear), you're better off. Similarly, unusual hairstyles or colors may bias an employer against you, rightly or wrongly. Make sure your hair is neat and acceptable (get a haircut?). Also go light on the makeup, self-tanning products, body scents, and other grooming agents. Don't wear a baseball cap or any other type of hat; and by all means, take off your sunglasses!

Beyond your physical appearance, you already know to be well bathed to minimize odor (leave your home early if you tend to sweat, so you can cool off in private), make good eye contact, smile, speak clearly using proper English, use good posture (don't slouch), offer a firm handshake, and arrive within five minutes of your interview. (If you're unsure of where you're going, "Mapquest" it and consider making a dry-run to the site so you won't be late.) First impressions can make or break your interview.

Remember Follow-Up

After your interview, send a thank you note. This thoughtful gesture will separate you from most of the other candidates. It demonstrates your ability to follow through, and it catches your prospective employer's attention one more time. In a 2005 Careerbuilder.com survey, nearly 15 percent of 650 hiring managers said they wouldn't hire someone who failed to send a thank you letter after the interview. Thirty-two percent say they would still consider the candidate, but would think less of him or her.

So do you hand write or e-mail the thank you letter? The fact is that format preferences vary. One in four hiring managers prefer to receive a thank you note in e-mail form only; 19 percent want the e-mail, followed up with a hard copy; 21 percent want a typed hard-copy only; and 23 percent prefer just a handwritten note. (Try to check with an assistant on the format your potential employer prefers.) Otherwise, sending an e-mail and a handwritten copy is a safe way to proceed.

Winning an Offer

There are no sweeter words to a job hunter than "We'd like to hire you." So naturally, when you hear them, you may be tempted to jump at the offer. *Don't.* Once an employer wants you, he or she will usually give you some time to make your decision and get any questions you may have answered. Now is the time to get specific about salary and benefits, and negotiate some of these points. If you haven't already done so, check out salary ranges for your position and area of the country on sites such as Payscale.com, Salary.com, and Salaryexpert.com (basic info is free; specific requests are not). Also, find out what sorts of benefits similar jobs offer. Then don't be afraid to negotiate in a diplomatic way. Asking for better terms is reasonable and expected. You may worry that asking the employer to bump up his offer may jeopardize your job, but handled intelligently, negotiating for yourself in fact may be a way to impress your future employer—and get a better deal for yourself.

After you've done all the hard work that successful job-hunting requires, you may be tempted to put your initiative into autodrive. However, the efforts you made to land your job-from clear communication to enthusiasm-are necessary now to pave your way to continued success. As Danielle Little, a human-resources assistant, says, "You must be enthusiastic and take the initiative. There is an urgency to prove yourself and show that you are capable of performing any and all related tasks. If your manager notices that you have potential, you will be given additional responsibilities, which will help advance your career." So do your best work on the job, and build your credibility. Your payoff will be career advancement and increased earnings.

Appendix B

Financial Aid

One major advantage of earning a two-year degree is that it is much less expensive than paying for a four-year school. Two years is naturally going to cost less than four, and two-year graduates enter the workplace and start earning a paycheck sooner than their four-year counterparts.

The latest statistics from the College Board show that average yearly total tuition and fees at a public two-year college is $2,191, compared to $5,491 at a four-year public college. That cost leaps to more than $21,000 on average for a year at a private four-year school.

With college costs relatively low, some two-year students overlook the idea of applying for financial aid at all. But the fact is, college dollars are available whether you're going to a trade school, community college, or university. About a third of all Pell Grants go to two-year public school students, and while two-year students receive a much smaller percentage of other aid programs, the funding is there for many who apply.

How Does Aid Work?

Financial aid comes in two basic forms: merit-based and need-based.

Merit-based awards are typically funds that recognize a particular talent or quality you may have, and they are given by private organizations, colleges, and the government. Merit-based awards range from scholarships for good writing to prizes for those who have shown promise in engineering. There are thousands of scholarships available for students who shine in academics, music, art, science, and more. Resources on how to get these awards are provided later in this chapter.

Need-based awards are given according to your ability to pay for college. In general, students from families that have less income and fewer assets receive more financial aid. To decide how much of this aid you qualify for, schools look at your family's income, assets, and other information regarding your finances. You provide this information on a financial aid form—usually the federal government's Free Application for Federal Student Aid (FAFSA). Based on the financial details you provide, the school of your choice calculates your Expected Family Contribution (EFC). This is the amount you are expected to pay toward your education each year.

Once your EFC is determined, a school uses this simple formula to figure out your financial aid package:

Cost of attendance at the school

- – Your EFC
- – Other outside aid (private scholarships)
- = Need

Schools put together aid packages that meet that need using loans, work-study, and grants.

Know Your School

When applying to a school, it's a good idea to find out their financial aid policy and history. Read over the school literature or contact the financial aid office and find out the following:

- ✔ *Is the school accredited?* Schools that are not accredited usually do not offer as much financial aid and are not eligible for federal programs.
- ✔ *What is the average financial aid package at the school?* The typical award size may influence your decision to apply or not.
- ✔ *What are all the types of assistance available?* Check if the school offers federal, state, private, or institutional aid.
- ✔ *What is the school's loan default rate?* The default rate is the percentage of students who took out federal student loans and failed to repay them on time. Schools that have a high default rate are often not allowed to offer certain federal aid programs.
- ✔ *What are the procedures and deadlines for submitting financial aid?* Policies can differ from school to school.
- ✔ *What is the school's definition of satisfactory academic progress?* To receive financial aid, you have to maintain your academic performance. A school may specify that you keep up at least a C+ or B average to keep getting funding.
- ✔ *What is the school's job placement rate?* The job placement rate is the percentage of students who find work in their field of study after graduating.

You'll want a school with a good placement rate so you can earn a good salary that may help you pay back any student loans you have.

Be In It to Win It

The key to getting the most financial aid possible is filling out the forms, and you have nothing to lose by applying. Most schools require that you file the FAFSA, which is *free* to submit, and you can even do it online. For more information on the FAFSA, visit the Web site at http://www.fafsa.ed.gov. If you have any trouble with the form, you can call 1-800-4-FED-AID for help.

To receive aid using the FAFSA, you must submit the form soon after January 1 prior to the start of your school year. A lot of financial aid is delivered on a first-come, first-served basis, so be sure to apply on time.

Filing for aid will require some work to gather your financial information. You'll need details regarding your assets and from your income tax forms, which include the value of all your bank accounts and investments. The form also asks if you have other siblings in college, the age of your parents, or if you have children. These factors can determine how much aid you receive.

Three to four weeks after you submit the FAFSA, you receive a document called the Student Aid Report (SAR). The SAR lists all the information you provided in the FAFSA and tells you how much you'll be expected to contribute toward school, or your Expected Family Contribution (EFC). It's important to review the information on the SAR carefully and make any corrections right away. If there are errors on this document, it can affect how much financial aid you'll receive.

The Financial Aid Package

Using information on your SAR, the school of your choice calculates your need (as described earlier) and puts together a financial aid package. Aid packages are often built with a combination of loans, grants, and work-study. You may also have won private scholarships that will help reduce your costs.

Keep in mind that aid awarded in the form of loans has to be paid back with interest just like a car loan. If you don't pay back according to agreed upon terms, you can go into *default*. Default usually occurs if you've missed payments for 180 days. Defaulted loans are often sent to collection agencies, which can charge costly fees and even take money owed out of your wages. Even worse, a defaulted loan is a strike on your credit history. If you have a negative credit history, lenders may deny you a mortgage, car loan, or other personal loan. There's also financial incentive for paying back on time—many lenders will give a 1 percent discount or more for students who make consecutive timely payments. The key is not to borrow more than you can afford. Know exactly how much your monthly payments will be on a loan when it comes due and estimate if those monthly payments will fit in your future budget. If you ever do run into trouble with loan payments, don't hesitate to contact your lender and see if you can come up with a new payment arrangement—lenders want to help you pay rather than see you go into default. If you have more than one loan, look into loan consolidation, which can lower overall monthly payments and sometimes lock in interest rates that are relatively low.

The Four Major Sources of Aid

U.S. Government Financial Aid

The federal government is the biggest source of financial aid. To find all about federal aid programs, visit http://www.studentaid.fed.gov or call 1-800-4-FED-AID with any questions. Download the free brochure *Funding Education Beyond High School*, which tells you all the details on federal programs. To get aid from federal programs you must be a regular student working toward a degree or certificate in an eligible program. You also have to have a high school diploma or equivalent, be a U.S. citizen or eligible non-citizen and have a valid Social Security number (check http://www.ssa.gov for info). If you are a male aged 18–25, you have to register for the Selective Service. (Find out more about that requirement at http://www.sss.gov or call 1-847-688-6888.) You must also certify that you are not in default on a student loan and that you will use your federal aid only for educational purposes.

Some specifics concerning federal aid programs can change a little each year, but the major programs are listed here and the fundamentals stay the same from year to year. (Note that amounts you receive generally depend on your enrollment status—whether it be full-time or part-time.)

Pell Grant
For students demonstrating significant need, this award has been ranging between $400 and $4,050. The size of a Pell grant does not depend on how much other aid you receive.

Supplemental Educational Opportunity Grant (SEOG)
Again for students with significant need, this award ranges from $100 to $4,000 a year. The size of the SEOG can be reduced according to how much other aid you receive.

Work-Study
The Federal Work-Study Program provides jobs for students showing financial need. The program encourages community service and work related to a student's course of study. You earn at least minimum wage and are paid at least once a month. Again, funds must be used for educational expenses.

Perkins Loans
With a low interest rate of 5 percent, this program lets students who can document the need borrow up to $4,000 a year.

Stafford Loans
These loans are available to all students regardless of need. However, students with need receive *subsidized* Staffords, which do not accrue interest while you're in school or in deferment. Students without need can take *unsubsidized* Staffords, which do accrue interest while you are in school or in deferment. Interest rates vary but can go no higher than 8.25 percent. Loan amounts vary too, according to what year of study you're in and whether you are financially dependent on your parents or not. Students defined as independent of their parents can borrow much more. (Students who have their own kids are also defined as independent. Check the exact qualifications for independent and dependent status on the federal government Web site http://www.studentaid.fed.gov.)

PLUS Loans
These loans for parents of dependent students are also available regardless of need. Parents with good credit can borrow up to the cost of attendance minus any other aid received. Interest rates are variable but can go no higher than 9 percent.

Tax Credits
Depending on your family income, qualified students can take federal tax deductions for education with maximums ranging from $1,500 to $2,000.

AmeriCorps
This program provides full-time educational awards in return for community service work. You can work before, during, or after your postsecondary education and use the funds either to pay current educational expenses or to repay federal student loans. Americorps participants work assisting teachers in Head Start, helping on conservation projects, building houses for the homeless, and doing other good works. For more information, visit http://www.AmeriCorps.gov

State Financial Aid
All states offer financial aid, both merit-based and need-based. Most states use the FAFSA to determine eligibility, but you'll have to contact your state's higher education agency to find out the exact requirements. You can get contact information for your state at http://www.bcol02.ed.gov/Programs/EROD/org_list.cfm. Most of the state aid programs are available only if you

study at a school in the state where you reside. Some states are very generous, especially if you're attending a state college or university. California's Cal Grant program gives needy state residents free tuition at in-state public universities.

School-Sponsored Financial Aid

The school you attend may offer its own loans, grants, and work programs. Many have academic- or talent-based scholarships for top-performing students. Some two-year programs offer cooperative education opportunities where you combine classroom study with off-campus work related to your major. The work gives you hands-on experience and some income, ranging from $2,500 to $15,000 per year depending on the program. Communicate with your school's financial aid department and make sure you're applying for the most aid you can possibly get.

Private Scholarships

While scholarships for students heading to four-year schools may be more plentiful, there are awards for the two-year students. Scholarships reward students for all sorts of talent—academic, artistic, athletic, technical, scientific, and more. You have to invest time hunting for the awards that you might qualify for. The Internet now offers many great scholarship search services. Some of the best ones are:

The College Board (http://www.collegeboard.com/pay)

FastWeb! (http://www.fastweb.monster.com)

MACH25 (http://www.collegenet.com)

Scholarship Research Network (http://www.srnexpress.com)

SallieMae's College Answer (http://www.collegeanswer.com)

Note: Be careful of scholarship-scam services that charge a fee for finding you awards but end up giving you nothing more than a few leads that you could have gotten for free with a little research on your own. Check out the Federal Trade Commission's Project ScholarScam (http://www.ftc.gov/bcp/conline/edcams/scholarship).

In your hunt for scholarship dollars, be sure to look into local community organizations (the Elks Club, Lions Club, PTA, etc.), local corporations, employers (your employer or your parents' may offer tuition assistance), trade groups, professional associations (National Electrical Contractors Association, etc.), clubs (Boy Scouts, Girl Scouts, Distributive Education Club of America, etc.), heritage organizations (Italian, Japanese,

Chinese, and other groups related to ethnic origin), church groups, and minority assistance programs.

Once you find awards you qualify for, you have to put in the time applying. This usually means filling out an application, writing a personal statement, and gathering recommendations.

General Scholarships

A few general scholarships for students earning two-year degrees are

Coca-Cola Scholars Foundation, Inc.

Coca-Cola offers 350 thousand-dollar scholarships (http://www.coca colascholars.org) per year specifically for students attending two-year institutions.

Phi Theta Kappa (PTK)

This organization is the International Honor Society of the Two-Year College. PTK is one of the sponsors of the All-USA Academic Team program, which annually recognizes 60 outstanding two-year college students (http://scholarships.ptk.org). First, Second, and Third Teams, each consisting of 20 members, are selected. The 20 First Team members receive stipends of $2,500 each. All 60 members of the All-USA Academic Team and their colleges receive extensive national recognition through coverage in *USA TODAY*. There are other great scholarships for two-year students listed on this Web site.

Hispanic Scholarship Fund (HSF)

HSF's High School Scholarship Program (http://www.hsf.net/scholar ship/programs/hs.php) is designed to assist high school students of Hispanic heritage obtain a college degree. It is available to graduating high school seniors who plan to enroll full-time at a community college during the upcoming academic year. Award amounts range from $1,000 to $2,500.

The Military

All branches of the military offer tuition dollars in exchange for military service. You have to decide if military service is for you. The Web site http://www.myfuture.com attempts to answer any questions you might have about military service.

Lower Your Costs

In addition to getting financial aid, you can reduce college expenses by being a money-smart student. Here are some tips.

Use Your Campus

Schools offer perks that some students never take advantage of. Use the gym. Take in a school-supported concert or movie night. Attend meetings and lectures with free refreshments.

Flash Your Student ID

Students often get discounts at movies, museums, restaurants, and stores. Always be sure to ask if there is a lower price for students and carry your student ID with you at all times. You can often save 10 to 20 percent on purchases.

Budget Your Funds

Writing a budget of your income and expenses can help you be a smart spender. Track what you buy on a budget chart. This awareness will save you dollars.

Share Rides

Commuting to school or traveling back to your hometown? Check and post on student bulletin boards for ride shares.

Buy Used Books

Used textbooks can cost half as much as new. Check your campus bookstore for deals and also try http://www.eCampus.com and http://www.bookcentral.com

Put Your Credit Card in the Freezer

That's what one student did to stop overspending. You can lock your card away any way you like, just try living without the ease of credit for awhile. You'll be surprised at the savings.

A Two-Year Student's Financial Aid Package

Minnesota State Colleges and Universities provides this example of how a two-year student pays for college. Note how financial aid reduces his out-of-pocket cost to about $7,000 per year.

Jeremy's Costs for One Year

Jeremy is a freshman at a two-year college in the Minnesota. He has a sister in college, and his parents own a home but have no other significant savings. His family's income: $42,000.

College Costs for One Year

Tuition	$3,437
Fees	$388
Estimated room and board*	$7,200
Estimated living expenses**	$6,116
Total cost of attendance	*$17,141*

Jeremy's Financial Aid

Federal grants (does not require repayment)	$2,800
Minnesota grant (does not require repayment)	$676
Work-study earnings	$4,000
Student loan (requires repayment)	$2,625
Total financial aid	*$10,101*
Total cost to Jeremy's family	***$7,040***

* Estimated cost reflecting apartment rent rate and food costs. The estimates are used to calculate the financial aid. If a student lives at home with his or her parents, the actual cost could be much less, although the financial aid amounts may remain the same.

** This is an estimate of expenses including transportation, books, clothing, and social activities.

Index